Environmentally Related Taxes in OECD Countries

ISSUES AND STRATEGIES

OECD

ORGANISATION FOR ECONOMIC CO-OPERATION AND DEVELOPMENT

ORGANISATION FOR ECONOMIC CO-OPERATION AND DEVELOPMENT

Pursuant to Article 1 of the Convention signed in Paris on 14th December 1960, and which came into force on 30th September 1961, the Organisation for Economic Co-operation and Development (OECD) shall promote policies designed:

- to achieve the highest sustainable economic growth and employment and a rising standard of living in Member countries, while maintaining financial stability, and thus to contribute to the development of the world economy;
- to contribute to sound economic expansion in Member as well as non-member countries in the process of economic development; and
- to contribute to the expansion of world trade on a multilateral, non-discriminatory basis in accordance with international obligations.

The original Member countries of the OECD are Austria, Belgium, Canada, Denmark, France, Germany, Greece, Iceland, Ireland, Italy, Luxembourg, the Netherlands, Norway, Portugal, Spain, Sweden, Switzerland, Turkey, the United Kingdom and the United States. The following countries became Members subsequently through accession at the dates indicated hereafter: Japan (28th April 1964), Finland (28th January 1969), Australia (7th June 1971), New Zealand (29th May 1973), Mexico (18th May 1994), the Czech Republic (21st December 1995), Hungary (7th May 1996), Poland (22nd November 1996), Korea (12th December 1996) and the Slovak Republic (14th December 2000). The Commission of the European Communities takes part in the work of the OECD (Article 13 of the OECD Convention).

Publié en français sous le titre :
LES TAXES LIÉES A L'ENVIRONNEMENT DANS LES PAYS DE L'OCDE
Problèmes et stratégies

FOREWORD

Economic instruments have been playing an increasing role in the environmental policies of OECD countries over the last decade, including environmentally related taxes. All OECD countries have introduced environmentally related taxes to some extent, and an increasing number are implementing comprehensive green tax reforms. Green tax reforms have been identified as a key framework condition for sustainable development in the recent OECD report *Sustainable Development: Critical Issues* and as a powerful tool for implementing the OECD *Environmental Strategy for the First Decade of the 21st Century* adopted by OECD environment ministers when they met in May 2001.

The current report describes the use of environmentally related taxes in OECD Member countries, and presents the growing evidence of their effectiveness as a means to reduce damage to the environment. It identifies obstacles to the broader use of such taxes, in particular fear of a loss of sectoral competitiveness or concerns about the distributional incidence of the policies, and suggests measures that can be taken to overcome such problems. Finally, the report discusses the issues and options relating to the taxing of greenhouse gases, an issue that is currently of particular importance to our Member countries.

Much remains to be done, however. In particular, governments must address the numerous exemptions that erode the environmental effectiveness of these taxes. The report concludes, *inter alia*, that further work is necessary for overcoming obstacles to policy reform and for a wider implementation of green tax reforms. This work includes the sharing of best practices and the consideration of possible concerted policy changes to be discussed at the OECD, but decided and implemented at the national level.

The report was prepared under the supervision of the Joint Meetings of Tax and Environment Experts, under the aegis of both the Committee on Fiscal Affairs and the Environment Policy Committee. A consultant, Rosalind Bark, prepared an initial draft and the final report was prepared by Jean-Philippe Barde and Nils Axel Braathen of the OECD Environment Directorate and Steven Clark and Chris Heady of the OECD Directorate for Financial, Fiscal and Enterprise Affairs.

Joke Waller-Hunter
Director, OECD Environment Directorate

William Witherell
Director, OECD Directorate for Financial,
Fiscal and Enterprise Affairs

3

TABLE OF CONTENTS

List of Boxes

List of Tables

List of Figures

SUMMARY AND CONCLUSIONS

i. Making taxation and environmental policies mutually reinforcing

OECD Member countries face a number of environmental challenges, including the protection of the ozone layer, local air quality, acidification and eutrophication, water supply and water quality, waste management and biodiversity losses. An issue currently high on the agenda in most Member countries is how to reduce greenhouse gas emissions in order to combat climate change and to meet the Kyoto Protocol commitments. Only a few Member countries are yet on track to fulfil these commitments. More generally, Member countries are increasingly concerned about the broader issues raised by sustainable development, and this was a main theme at the OECD's 2001 Ministerial Council meeting.[1]

Over the last decade, economic instruments have been playing a growing role in environmental policies of OECD countries. In this context, a distinctive feature is the increasing role of environmentally related taxes. All countries have introduced environmental taxes to a varying extent, and an increasing number of countries are implementing comprehensive green-tax reforms, while others are contemplating to do so. Depending on design features, environmental taxes support the "polluter pays principle", under which the costs of pollution prevention and control should be reflected in the price and output of goods and services which cause pollution as a result of their production and/or consumption. However, obviously, many factors other than the use of economic instruments also affect levels of pollution in a given country.

The revenue from environmentally related taxes averages roughly 2% of GDP in Member countries.[2] These taxes are introduced in support of a number of policy objectives, where policy choices typically depend on a balancing of conflicting goals. In the context of environmental concerns, environmentally related taxes introduce a price signal that helps ensure that polluters take into account the costs of pollution on the environment when they make production and consumption decisions. Taxes are a flexible policy instrument that can minimise control costs for achieving a given pollution target and provide incentives for technological innovation and further reductions in polluting emissions.

Taxes on the purchase or use of motor vehicles and fuels, including taxes on petrol and diesel, generate most of the revenues from environmentally related taxes. In some countries taxes are also used to address a broad spectre of other environmental problems. Nevertheless, in many countries there is scope for expanding the use of environmentally related taxes.

There is growing evidence on the effectiveness of environmentally related taxes in OECD countries as a means to reduce damage to the environment. Available evidence indicates that the responsiveness of demand to changes in the price of, for example, energy often is significantly higher in the long run than in the short run, implying that a consistent long term implementation of environmentally related taxes could reduce energy consumption and improve the environment. There are also indications that adjustments of tax rates for competing energy sources can cause significant fuel-switching to take place if tax rates on energy products are re-modulated according to environmental criteria.

Green-tax reforms can be implemented by a series of complementary measures, such as restructuring existing taxes, for example on energy or transport, to reflect the polluting characteristics of the different products or activities, or introducing new taxes, *e.g.* on water use and water pollution, waste, certain chemicals, etc. It is also most important to remove or adjust environmentally harmful fiscal provisions, such as tax exemptions or subsidies having detrimental effects on the environment, while giving due notice to the non-environmental objectives the provisions were meant to serve.

The circumstances that impact on the design of the tax system differ between countries. So does the environmental situation and the sources of environmental problems within countries. Countries also differ in contribution to regional and global environmental problems, for which international co-operation is necessary. In the context of current structural adjustment and regulatory reform in OECD economies, countries should consider the opportunities and potential for greening their fiscal systems, according to their specific economic, fiscal and environmental situation.

ii. Implementing environmentally related taxes

When implementing environmentally related taxes, the environmental (and other) objectives of the policy measure should be clearly stated from the outset.[3] When deciding on a particular measure, each country should carefully review the range of measures that could potentially be used to achieve those objectives. A thorough analysis of the costs and benefits of each approach, and an assessment of current practices, should be carried out in order to evaluate the relative merits of the alternative measures.

Often environmentally related taxes can be usefully implemented in the context of policy packages, *i.e.* in combination with other policy instruments, such as voluntary approaches, command and control regulations, and tradable permits. The potential for such policy packages should be analysed further.

ii.1. International competitiveness

A major obstacle to the implementation of environmentally related taxes in certain cases is the fear of reduced international competitiveness in the most polluting, often energy intensive, sectors of the economy. To date, environmentally related taxes currently imposed by OECD countries have not been identified as causing significant reductions in the competitiveness of any sector, although this can in part be due to the fact that Countries applying environmentally related taxes have provided for total or partial exemptions for energy intensive industries. Indeed, the OECD/EU database shows that environmentally related taxes are levied almost exclusively on households and the transport sector. These exemptions and rebates create inefficiencies in pollution abatement and undermine application of the polluter pays principle (PPP). The finding is also consistent with research on economic performance that shows that skills and capital investment largely determine sectoral competitiveness. Further, different sectors within countries differ in terms of their exposure to international trade and competition.

Blanket exemptions for polluting products along with rebates for heavy polluting industries can significantly reduce the effectiveness of environmentally related taxes in curbing pollution and similarly reduce incentives for developing and introducing new technologies.

This report suggests several options for a more effective imposition of environmentally related taxes without reducing the given country's competitiveness. Consideration might for instance be given to a dual (two-tier) rate structure, rather than the use of full exemptions, with lower rates for the more internationally exposed sectors, as a possible alternative. The negative environmental effect of exemptions and rate reductions can also be limited by ensuring that firms that currently benefit from exemptions and reduced tax rates sign up to stringent mitigation measures. Furthermore, in instances where exemptions and rebates are currently given for competitiveness reasons, countries examining revenue recycling as an option should consider imposing environmental taxes on industry while introducing innovative methods to channel part of the environmental tax revenues back to industry in such a way that marginal abatement incentives are not reduced.

Pre-announcing the introduction of environmentally related taxes and tax rate increases, and a gradual reduction or phasing out of rebates and exemptions, are two policy options that could ease implementation, make environmental taxes more effective, while also addressing competitiveness concerns. In some countries, there is also scope for improving the design of tax provisions to ensure that any remaining exemptions and refund mechanisms are properly targeted to achieve their stated objectives. Careful design and targeting would reduce the economic costs of achieving a given environmental target, including obligations of countries under the Kyoto Protocol.

Countries would also benefit from exploring better integration of environmentally motivated reforms of their fiscal systems with broader fiscal reforms. It is the combined effects of these reforms that will determine the impacts on sectoral and nation-wide competitiveness. Possible negative competitiveness impacts on some sectors from the environmentally related part of a broader reform might thus be reduced. And while some sectors may face a net loss in competitiveness if countries expand environmentally related taxation unilaterally, other more environmentally benign sectors of the economy could improve their competitiveness, *inter alia* depending on how revenues generated in the reform are redistributed.

Alternative policy instruments used to reduce environmental pollution, such as regulations, would also affect firm's costs and impact on the competitiveness position of individual sectors and the country as a whole. By enhancing the economic efficiency by which a given target is reached, properly designed environmentally related taxes will help minimise adverse effects on competitiveness nation-wide.

One way to address international competitiveness concerns is for countries to share information, experiences and best practices as regards possible options and opportunities for expanding the application of environmentally related taxes. Countries concerned with competitiveness implications of adjusting certain environmentally related taxes on a unilateral basis could consider possible concerted policy options and changes, decided and implemented at the national level, but within a framework which provides for a multilateral dialogue. The OECD provides a unique forum to facilitate such policy discussions, bringing together tax and environment experts from the governments of 30 developed countries while also providing an extensive outreach programme which now covers over 60 non-member countries.

ii.2. Income distribution

The distributional incidence of environmental policy measures has become a key issue in the policy debate. The data show that some environmentally related taxes can be regressive at least to some extent, impacting more on low-income households, and can also increase regional income disparities in some countries. However, a complete assessment of distributional effects would also include the secondary impact of any compensation payments, tax reductions, and the induced employment effects. It should also take into account the distribution of the environmental benefits resulting from the tax.

Mitigation measures (*e.g.* reduced tax rates for lower incomes) to address the regressivity concerns can reduce the environmental effectiveness of the taxes. Governments should seek other, and more direct, measures if low-income households are to be compensated (*e.g.*, transfers). Such compensation measures can maintain the price signal of the tax, whilst reducing the impact of the tax on household income.

ii.3. The use of tax revenue

Each country decides on the use of revenues from environmentally related taxes according to its specific economic, fiscal and environmental situation. Several options are available. The revenues could alleviate a budget deficit, contribute to a budget surplus, or finance discretionary increases in government expenditures. The revenues can also provide room for discretionary reductions in other taxes to reduce distortions (efficiency losses) in labour or capital markets, address competitiveness concerns, or to increase public acceptance of environmental taxes. Certain forms of spending and tax reductions have the potential to undermine the PPP principle, and therefore require careful consideration.

Where the revenues are earmarked to specific spending purposes, some of this allocation may be environmentally motivated. In some cases, earmarking of part of the revenues might enhance the environmental effectiveness or economic efficiency of the tax in question. Earmarking, however, may violate the polluter pays principle. Further, earmarking revenues fixes the use of tax revenue in advance, which may create an obstacle for the re-evaluation and modification of the tax and spending programs. Therefore, the economic and environmental rationale of such measures should be evaluated regularly to avoid inefficient spending that would otherwise not be financed from general tax revenues. For instance, allocating transport taxes to road infrastructure may lead to over-investment in that sector.

Revenues can also be used to enable reductions in other taxes. This can reduce the efficiency loss generally incurred by the collection of tax revenues if the taxes being reduced are more distorting than the environmentally related taxes being introduced. This question depends on the final incidence of the taxes in question, where different taxes may have different tax burden effects.[4]

One particular, and often debated option, is a shifting of the tax burden from labour to pollution, with the expectation that a lower tax burden on labour would encourage work effort and thereby contribute to a decrease in unemployment, while improving the environment (the "double dividend" hypothesis). The theoretical and empirical evidence for a double dividend is not conclusive. Nevertheless, a number of governments are implementing revenue-neutral green tax reform, *inter alia* with the intention of realising a double dividend. If it could be demonstrated conclusively that positive employment effects follow from switching the burden of taxation to pollution from labour, this evidence could counterbalance the competitiveness and equity arguments used against implementing new or higher environmentally related taxes. There is a need to carry out *ex post* evaluations of these policies, *inter alia* to reject or confirm the double dividend hypothesis.

ii.4. Acceptance building

Building acceptance is a key condition for effective green-tax reforms. Given this, countries may wish to pursue several complementary efforts including identifying, simply and clearly, the objectives behind an environmentally related tax, disseminating information, and allowing sufficient time for public hearings or other forms of consultation. This could include the creation of "green tax commissions" and inter-ministerial working parties. A period for consultation enables public and private stakeholder groups to influence policy and the government to explain wider policy objectives behind contemplated reforms. Such involvement lends public legitimacy and support to environmental efforts. In some cases, public acceptance of an increase in environmentally related taxation can be enhanced if, at the same time, increased spending on related issues is announced, or by the use of policy packages (see page 10).

As noted above, where exemptions and rebates from environmentally related taxes have been previously granted to industry to encourage acceptance of a given environmental program in response to perceived competitiveness concerns, alternative means to build acceptance should be considered, including innovative options for revenue recycling to industry without removing marginal abatement incentives. Generally, such measures should be implemented on a provisional and transitory basis.

iii. Further work

The joint meetings have identified the following possible tasks for further OECD work:

- Annual updates of the database on environmentally related taxes. Consideration should also be given to extending the database to include a fuller coverage of relevant fees and charges, in addition to environmentally related taxes, and perhaps to incorporate information concerning the proportion of the potential tax base (*e.g.*, emissions, energy use, waste) covered by full rate taxes and the proportion covered by reduced tax rates and exemptions.

- More extensive analyses of the material contained in the database and discussion of how to use the database for policy analysis and subsequently for formulating policies and measures.

- Continue surveys and assessments of ongoing "green fiscal reforms" in Member countries. Member countries should be encouraged to commit additional resources to the assessment (*ex ante* and *ex post*) of environmental taxes, including design features as regards the taxation of industry, obstacles to the use of environmental instruments and how to overcome them, and revenue recycling effects, including the realisation of any "double dividend".

- Review and assess empirical evidence for competitiveness impacts identified as an important obstacle for the widespread use of uniform environmentally related taxes – and the various policy options to compensate such impacts.

- Undertake research on the combined implementation of taxes and other instruments (tradable permits, voluntary agreements, etc.) used by different countries in the pursuit of common environmental goals.

- Organise meetings of senior tax and environment experts from OECD governments interested in environmentally related taxation to facilitate a sharing of information, experiences and best practices. Such meetings should explore options and opportunities to enhance the application of and reduce exemptions to environmentally related taxes, and offer parties a forum for considering possible concerted policy changes, decided at the national level, to address international competitiveness concerns in certain areas. Such work should build upon efforts undertaken by the UN and at the European Union level.

- Through the OECD outreach programme, share information, experiences and best practices with non-member countries.

NOTES

1. The Communiqué of the 16-17 Mai 2001 Ministerial Council meeting stated *inter alia* that "The implementation of instruments such as tradable permit systems, environment-related taxes, and the phasing out of support programmes that are environmentally damaging in agriculture, fisheries, transport, energy, manufacturing and elsewhere, should be pursued, and applied according to national circumstances". "OECD will continue to assist governments by ... identifying how *obstacles to policy reforms*, in particular to the better use of market-based instruments, and to the reduction of environmentally harmful subsidies, can be overcome; and deepening its analytical work on these instruments."

2. See the OECD/EU database on environmentally related taxes and charges, available at *www.oecd.org/env/policies/ taxes/index.htm*.

3. Existing energy taxes may play valid roles in environmental policies, even where environmentally related objectives were not explicitly given in the introduction or maintenance of these taxes.

4. All taxes, including taxes imposed on pollution, are ultimately borne by individuals as consumers, workers, employers or investors. However, final tax incidence – that is, how its burden gets passed on to individuals through some combination of higher prices, lower wages, and/or lower returns to capital – can differ depending on the specific tax and the characteristics of the affected markets.

INTRODUCTION

Environmental issues continue to rank high on the political agenda of many Member countries and also figure prominently in work at the OECD. In 1991 the OECD initiated work on taxation and the environment with the creation of a Task Force on Taxation and Environment, under the supervision of the Committee on Fiscal Affairs (CFA) and the Environment Policy Committee (EPOC). In 1993 the Task Force released its findings in a report entitled *Taxation and the Environment Complementary Policies* [OECD (1993)]. These findings were elaborated on by a special Joint Sessions on Taxation and Environment, with a 1995 report; *Environmental Taxes in OECD Countries* [OECD (1995a)]. The main findings from this initial work by the Task Force and Joint Sessions can be found in the report *Implementation Strategies for Environmental Taxes* [OECD (1996)]. In May 1997 the OECD Council agreed to the derestriction of a report "Environmental Taxes and Green Tax Reform", with a request for carrying out further work in this area.

The Joint Meetings on Taxation and Environment approved a work plan for the development of a database of environmentally related taxes and charges and the writing of this report on *Environmentally Related Taxation in OECD Countries: Issues and Strategies*. The OECD/EU database on environmentally related taxes is available at *www.oecd.org/env/policies/taxes/index.htm*.[1] The database not only provides information on environmentally related taxes by country and by specific tax-base, but also information on tax rebates and exemptions. In addition in preparation for this report, the Secretariat prepared a questionnaire on the practical implementation and assessment of environmentally related taxes. This report builds on the database and the responses to the questionnaire and other relevant sources of information.

The on-going efforts of OECD countries to "green' their tax systems are important. There have been significant developments and this report highlights lessons learned and the main challenges countries face when they consider whether to modify existing or introduce new environmentally related taxes. Evidence for the environmental effectiveness of taxes is reviewed and recommendations are made on how to improve the effectiveness and the acceptability of environmentally related taxation. This is particularly timely given the need to formulate workable, environmentally effective, and cost effective policies in order to meet the Kyoto Protocol greenhouse gas emission commitments.

Environmentally related taxes

The environmental effect of a tax comes primarily through the impact it has on relative consumer and producer prices of environmentally related goods and services, in conjunction with the relevant price elasticities (see Section 8.1). For example, a tax on heating fuels introduced primarily for fiscal reasons will have the same environmental impacts as a tax on heating fuels introduced primarily to combat CO_2 emissions – to the extent that the tax leads to similar changes in the prices of heating fuels. Therefore, for the purpose of this report, an environmentally related *tax* is defined as any compulsory, *unrequited* payment to general government levied on tax-bases deemed to be of particular environmental relevance. Taxes are unrequited in the sense that benefits provided by government to taxpayers are not normally in proportion to their payments.

Fees and *charges* are examples of *requited* payments to the government; they are levied more or less in proportion to services provided (*e.g.* the level of wastes collected and treated), are also to some extent included in the tax database, and are – when appropriate – taken into account in this report. The term levy can be used to cover taxes, fees and charges.

Taxes and charges are only one type of market based instrument available to the policymaker. Other economic measures are auctioned and non-auctioned tradable emission permits, deposit-refund schemes, performance bonds, non-compliance fees and environmentally motivated subsidies. All these instruments differ from command and control regulation in that they provide an incentive to polluters to modify their production or consumption behaviour via price signals. One of the theoretical advantages of economic instruments is that economic agents have the flexibility to choose how to respond to the price signal, and the assumption is that they do so at least-cost and therefore efficiently and, in addition, the allocation of pollution reducing effort among firms is efficient.

When implementing new policy measures, the environmental (and other) objectives of the measure should be clearly stated from the outset. In some cases, the objectives pursued can be conflicting. For instance, policies aiming to lower NO_x emissions can in some cases cause increased greenhouse gas emissions. There can also be conflicts between environmental policy objectives and objectives related to economic development, competitiveness of certain industrial sectors, regional employment possibilities, etc. Often environmentally related taxes can be usefully implemented in the context of policy packages, *i.e.* in combination with other policy instruments, such as voluntary approaches, command and control regulations, and tradable permits. Modifications to existing taxes, for instance on energy, may also be an option, even where environmentally related objectives were not explicitly given these taxes were introduced. When deciding on a particular measure, each country should carefully review the range of measures that could potentially be used to achieve those objectives. A thorough analysis of the costs and benefits of each approach and an assessment of current practices should be carried out in order to evaluate the relative merits of the alternative measures.

There are links between the polluter pays principle (PPP) and environmentally related taxation.[2] The OECD definition of the PPP as expressed in the 1972 OECD Guiding Principles on the International Economic Aspects of Environmental Policies, reads:

"The principle to be used for allocating costs of pollution prevention and control measures to encourage rational use of scarce environmental resources and to avoid distortions in international trade and investment is the so-called 'Polluter Pays Principle'. This principle means that the polluter should bear the expenses of carrying out the above mentioned measures decided by public authorities to ensure that the environment is in an acceptable state. In other words, the costs of these measures should be reflected in the cost of goods and services which cause pollution in production and/or consumption. Such measures should not be accompanied by subsidies that would create significant distortions in international trade and investment."

In this context, the PPP is a non-subsidisation principle, meaning simply that governments should not as a general rule give subsidies to their industries for pollution control. It is intended to guide the allocation of costs between the government and the private sector in paying for domestic pollution or protecting their national environments. It concerns *who* should pay for environmental protection, not *how much* should be paid.

Outline of the report

The report is divided into two parts:

- Part I provides a brief theory of environmentally related taxation, the options for Green Tax Reform, including a discussion of the double dividend issue, and how to evaluate the performance of such taxes. The scope for using environmentally related taxation in policy packages is also discussed.

- Part II addresses how the OECD countries have managed the contentious issues of competitiveness and income distribution in current environmentally related taxation. The part ends with a discussion of how such taxes might contribute to meeting Kyoto Protocol greenhouse gas emission commitments and with an assessment of current use of environmentally related taxes.

NOTES

1. Forum for the Future, London, has in a separate project prepared another database on environmental taxes in the European Union Member States, plus Norway and Switzerland, for the European Commission. This database can be accessed at *http://europa.eu.int/comm/environment/enveco/env_database/database.htm.*
2. This paragraph is based on OECD (1995*b*).

Part I

CONCEPTUAL BACKGROUND

Chapter 1

A BRIEF THEORY OF ENVIRONMENTALLY RELATED TAXATION[1]

1.1. Externalities

The basic theoretical premise behind the introduction of environmental instruments, including environmentally related taxation, to correct for environmental damage is the existence of negative environmental externalities in unregulated economies. A negative externality is a cost that one economic agent imposes on another but does not take into account when making production or consumption decisions. When the costs of pollution or resource use are not reflected in prices, market inefficiencies result with excessive production or consumption of products and activities that impose social costs. Externalities exist because of the public goods nature of the environment. In the absence of property rights for clean air, clean water, etc. economic agents use these services without regard for the impact their decisions have on other economic agents, including future generations. Even where charges and taxes are raised on a polluting activity, for example on municipal waste disposal, often they do not fully internalise the cost of the externality. Where environmental costs are fully internalised into the price of a product or activity a reallocation of resources in the economy occurs according to fair and efficient prices.

Figure 1 depicts a highly simplified economic model to illustrate externality effects and the role of corrective taxation.[2] In theory, an efficient level of a given polluting activity (*e.g.*, mineral processing) is reached where the marginal benefit (MB) from emitting an additional unit of pollution (or viewed alternatively, not restricting pollution by an additional unit), measured in terms of abatement costs avoided at the margin, just equals its marginal social cost (MSC) of that activity. The latter consists of the private marginal cost (MC) plus the marginal environmental cost (MEC) of an additional unit of

Figure 1. **The socially efficient level of taxation**

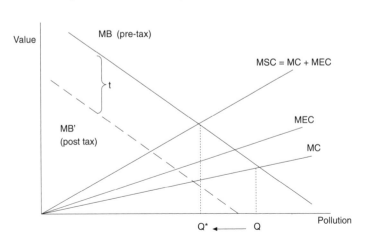

21

pollution, which is assumed to increase with the total pollution emitted. Under an unregulated market, the private result yields pollution activity in the amount Q, at the point where the marginal benefit schedule (which slopes downward to the right, reflecting lower abatement costs per unit at higher pollution levels) just equals the private marginal cost of pollution.[3] The Pigouvian solution to reduce pollution to the social optimum at Q* is to introduce an indirect tax at rate t per unit of pollution. The optimal tax rate t is shown to be the vertical distance between the MSC and MC schedules, equal to the marginal environmental cost of pollution at the social optimum Q*. The introduction of the tax shifts the marginal benefit curve down to MB', resulting in a new private equilibrium at Q*. The socially optimal level of pollution is realised by internalising the environmental damage in the private market decision, with that damage captured by the environmental tax.

1.2. Economic instruments

Unlike command and control regulation, economic instruments – environmentally related taxes, charges and tradable emission permits – create direct price signals for producers and consumers for environmental resource scarcities and the costs of pollution. Higher relative prices for polluting products and activities impacts on consumers' consumption decisions, including the choice between different products and activities. Economic instruments also create incentives for industry to abate pollution and to restructure away from producing polluting products and from polluting production methods, thereby reducing pollution without "abating".

Environmentally related taxation is one policy instrument that can be used to ensure that some, if not all, of the externality costs, the costs to the environment, are internalised (or "priced" into) the decision-making process. For example, in designing a policy to reduce carbon dioxide (CO_2) emissions a policymaker could either tax the emissions directly, thereby setting the price – but not the quantity – of the emissions, or he could issue or sell emission permits that set the quantity – but not the price – of pollution abatement. In practice, the quantity "guarantee" delivered by tradable emission permits is subject to the level of the penalties for non-compliance, and its detection. Alternatively, energy-efficiency standards for industry, households, and transport could be enforced or industry could be encouraged to sign voluntary agreements with the government. These agreements may for instance specify certain emission targets, but not the means for reaching these targets [see OECD (1999a)]. The comparative efficiency of these various policy options is discussed in theory in Section 2.6.

1.3. Static efficiency

The theoretical advantage of economic instruments compared to command and control regulation is that there are opportunities to realise static and dynamic efficiencies. The static efficiencies can be realised at the level of abatement measures undertaken by industry, the impact on consumer decisions, and industry structure.

Command and control regulation often takes the form of uniform emission standards across an industry because regulators lack the necessary information about firm-specific pollution abatement costs to design an efficient pattern of abatement among regulated firms, i.e. a pattern where the marginal abatement costs between firms are equalised. However, taxing emissions with a common tax rate across all sources, or setting up a tradable emission permit scheme, equalises the marginal abatement costs (static efficiency) between polluters. In this way economic instruments provide incentives for efficient abatement measures across industry, with those industries that face lower abatement costs cutting back on pollution emissions relatively more. Firms have the flexibility either to abate another unit of pollution, if the cost of this abatement activity is less than the emission tax, or the emission permit price, while if the marginal abatement cost is high, they can pay the tax or buy an emission permit. Therefore those firms that have the lowest abatement costs undertake the most pollution abatement, and those firms that would have found it costly to reduce emissions to meet a uniform pollution reduction, can opt to pay the tax, or buy emission permits. The result is that abatement is achieved at minimum total cost and marginal abatement costs are equalised between firms. Economic instruments create flexibility and incentives that result in a least-cost pattern of abatement.

Environmental taxes and auctioned permits also operate to reduce pollution through their effect on relative prices. This occurs because increased production costs resulting from these policy instruments get partially or fully reflected in higher consumer prices on goods and services that are harmful to the environment. Thus consumers are encouraged to substitute away from these outputs, with demand shifting in favour of lower priced alternatives that are less environmentally damaging. Related to this is the fact that reduced demand for harmful products will encourage industrial restructuring. In particular, by imposing higher environmentally related costs on production activities and sectors that impose greater environmental damage, capital and labour would be encouraged to shift over time towards more environmentally friendly businesses.

1.4. Dynamic efficiency[4]

Another advantage of economic instruments is the incentives they create for dynamic efficiency, *i.e.* an ongoing incentive to reduce pollution abatement costs. To comply with command and control regulation firms must meet set emission limits or use specific technologies, but they have no incentive to reduce emissions beyond the set limits. In contrast, taxes create a continual incentive for firms to further reduce polluting emissions, through cost-effective abatement, innovation of cleaner production techniques and better abatement technologies, and through industrial restructuring. Consumers also have incentives to demand less polluting products and to reduce polluting activities. The specificity of a tax requires polluters to pay for residual emissions on top of abatement costs. It is this key feature, illustrated in Figure 2 below, that provides incentives for dynamic efficiency.

In Figure 2, the areas A and B, under the initial marginal abatement cost curve (MAC_1), represent the abatement costs of reducing emissions to E_1. The areas C, D and E show the tax payment the polluter must continue to make for all remaining emissions, *i.e.* 0-E_1. It is the on-going tax payments for these permitted emissions that creates a dynamic incentive for further pollution abatement, and innovation to reduce costs. It is also these tax payments that generate industry opposition to environmentally related taxation, because firms subject to alternative environmental policy instruments, for example grandfathered (freely allocated) emission permits, negotiated agreements, and regulations, only pay abatement costs, not also the tax on the remaining emissions.

Figure 2. **The dynamic efficiency of taxes**

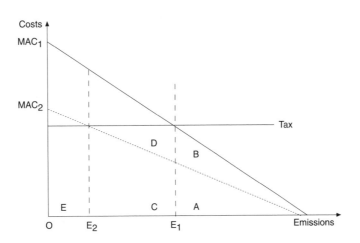

A tax creates incentives to further reduce pollution when abatement costs decline. For instance, if technical progress lowers the cost of marginal abatement, from MAC_1 to MAC_2, and the tax remains at the same level; the firm will reduce emissions to E_2. The firm will save areas B and D in reduced abatement costs and also area C in reduced tax payments. Area E equals the residual tax payments. However, with an emission standard set at E_1, a technological improvement that lowered abatement costs from MAC_1 to MAC_2 would not provide incentives to reduce emissions beyond E_1. The polluter saves area B in abatement costs, but has no incentive to reduce emissions.

1.5. Tax design issues

In practice, the design and implementation of environmentally related taxation is likely to differ from simple textbook discussions. For example, such taxes may be introduced to simply raise revenue, in which case the same environmental considerations and linkages determining the optimal tax rate generally would not apply. Where environmental goals are a central objective, measurement and estimation difficulties can be expected in practice, for example in linking a specific tax to the amount of environmental damage. Political concerns, including for example concerns over industrial competitiveness and income (re)distribution, may also figure prominently and need to be assessed (see Chapters 4 and 5).

1.5.1. *Tax-bases and tax rates*

In designing an environmentally related tax, careful description of the tax base is required to minimise negative environmental or economic consequences. To illustrate, waste taxes need to be carefully designed to avoid increased deposition of waste at unregulated, tax exempt sites. Box 1 describes the relationship between taxes and tax-bases.

Box 1. Taxes and tax-bases

It is important to understand the difference between *taxes* and *tax-bases*. When the terms *taxes*, *fees* and *charges* are used, reference is made to the individual legal act that governs the levy in question, for example the "Tax on mineral oils" or the "Tax on registration of motor vehicles" adopted by the national parliament.

A given tax is levied on one or several tax-bases, with (often) varying tax rates. For example, in the case of a "Tax on mineral oils", separate tax rates could be levied on the tax-bases "leaded petrol", "unleaded petrol", "diesel with normal sulphur content", "diesel with low sulphur content", etc. A "Tax on registration of motor vehicles" could include separate tax rates for a long list of different tax-bases, such as passenger cars of different types and/or sizes, lorries of different types and sizes, etc.

Strictly speaking, terms like "fee-base" and "charge-base" ought to be used when talking about the goods or services on which fees or charges are levied. These terms are however seldom used, and in this publication the term "tax-base" is used whenever reference is made to the base on which a given tax, fee or charge is levied.

Source: Braathen (2000).

In practice environmentally related taxation is introduced for various reasons, for example, to introduce incentives to reduce polluting activity and waste, to slow resource depletion, as a new tax base, or to meet multiple objectives (*i.e.* environmental *and* fiscal). Correspondingly there are different mechanisms for deciding the rate of the environmentally related tax. Tax rates could be chosen so as to seek to internalise fully the environmental costs of pollution. Externality evaluation using benefit-cost analysis supported the choice of tax rates for the 1996 UK landfill tax[5] [CSERGE (1993)] and also the planned tax rates on the UK extraction of aggregates from quarries [Pearce and Barbier (2000)]. Rates can be set to secure the fulfilment of a given environmental target, *e.g.* Kyoto greenhouse gas targets. Alternatively rates could be chosen independently of environmental considerations, *i.e.* to raise revenue, nevertheless such taxation would still have an environmental impact.

1.5.2. *Points of taxation and linkage*

A principle of good environmentally related taxation is to tax the behaviour to be influenced as directly as possible, in order to enhance the chance of actually influencing behaviour. However, in practice it can be costly and difficult to measure (or estimate) emissions, if there are several different pollutants; if the pollutant affects several different media, (*i.e.* SO_2 emissions damage air, land, and water environments); and if emissions are generated by many, small, mobile sources. A proxy for pollution can then be used; for instance taxing vehicle emissions based on average fuel consumption, not measured emissions.

The information requirements to ensure strong linkage between a tax and the environmental damage can be demanding. For example, a product tax should ideally be based on an assessment of the total environmental impact of the product over its life-cycle, from production through consumption to disposal. In addition, the evaluation should include information on the possibilities for alternative, less polluting production methods and substitute products, the prospects for displacing pollution to another medium, and estimates of any positive or negative side-effects. A number of environmental assessments for different products and activities have been undertaken, providing information on which to base good environmentally related tax practice.

It is important when designing a tax to choose an appropriate point of taxation. In general environmentally related taxes are imposed on one of the following: on the sale of final goods to consumers (consumption taxes); on producers, in relation to their output; and on producers, either on measured or estimated emissions or on inputs in business activities (in production or processing). Taxes on products (at final or intermediate stages of production) can be imposed per unit, or according to pollution characteristics (*e.g.*, carbon or sulphur content in fuels, materials used in packaging, etc.). Consumption taxes ensure that consumers face the price signal and therefore have incentives to change their consumption patterns away from polluting products. Emissions taxes levied on industry create incentives for industry to either abate emissions or to switch to cleaner inputs, products or production technology. Taxes can also be levied on resource use, for example on the use of mineral aggregates, or on resource rents, *i.e.* excess profits made selling mineral oil products.

1.5.3. *Pre-announcements*

A number of governments, for example Denmark, France, Germany, Italy, and United Kingdom, have pre-announced new and/or higher environmentally related taxes. The benefit of such a pre-announcement strategy is that it should increase the behavioural effects of the tax, by giving a degree of planning certainty and a perception of greater permanence of the tax, thereby improving the longer-term signals to the taxpayer to adjust his consumption, production and investment.

1.6. Options for the use of tax revenues

Unlike policy instruments such as regulations and non-auctioned tradable emission permits, environmentally related taxes raise revenue. This raises questions regarding the optimal use(s) of those revenues, taking into account the implementing country's fiscal position, existing tax distortions and evidence on efficiency gains from alternative tax mixes, and the desire to guard environmental and/or other intended incentives under the tax system. Concerns over the level of support for (or resistance to) environmental taxes may also factor in.

1.6.1. *General budget and earmarking*

Revenue from environmentally related taxes can be paid into the general government budget, and its use determined by wider policy issues. The revenues could contribute to a budget surplus or alleviate a budget deficit, provide room for discretionary increases in government expenditures, or discretionary reductions in other taxes. These options have been studied in detail in a number of reports. For example, a Japanese study [EIEP (2000)] simulated the impact of three different options for spending carbon tax revenue (increasing public expenditure and boosting public reserves, reducing public debt, and cutting income tax) whilst achieving a 2% cut in CO_2 emissions by 2010 from 1990 levels. The study indicated that the policy of reducing public debt, which reduced interest rates and shifted money to the private sector, would result in the least negative impact on the economy.

Alternatively, the revenue might be earmarked to specific spending purposes, some of which may be environmentally motivated. Earmarking programmes may, however, be contrary to the polluter pays principle. Whether or not a given polluter faces an increased burden as a result of a given environmentally related tax depends on whether earmarked expenditures benefit that polluter or not, and if they do, to what extent (a net burden may still be imposed). Revenues can also be allocated to targeted reductions in other taxes (see Section 1.6.2).

There are many examples of earmarked revenues in waste management and water management, although in these examples, charges rather than taxes raise most revenue. Taxes can also be earmarked, for example fuel taxes are often earmarked for road building. The OECD/EU database on environmentally related taxes illustrates numerous earmarked levies: 65 different taxes in 18 countries and 109 fees and charges in 23 countries.

There are disadvantages to earmarking revenues. First, earmarking fixes the use of tax revenue in advance, which creates obstacles for a re-evaluation based on economic and environmental rationale of a targeted expenditure programme financed by earmarked revenues, and the frequent result is inefficient spending of government revenue. For instance, allocating transport taxes to road infrastructure may lead to over-investment in that sector. Second, earmarking creates inflexibility; programmes may last longer than is optimal because of bureaucratic and other vested interests' obstruction to reform, even when policy priorities have changed.

However, environmental advantages might result from the earmarking of environmental revenues. For example, Andersen (1999) concludes in his comparative study on the clean water policies in four OECD countries that one factor behind the success of the Dutch system of water related charges compared to the Danish and Belgium systems, was the earmarking of revenue. The process by which revenue was earmarked in the Netherlands improved co-operation among polluters and between specialised water institutions and polluters and regulators, that may have resulted in lower transaction costs in implementing and investing in effective pollution reduction. Andersen argues that the "availability of information and advice, and the opportunities for financial assistance on the basis of the proceeds of the levies, smoothed the transition" to a reduced pollution outcome. Earmarking revenues may also improve the political acceptability of taxes because of the dedicated nature of expenditures, a proportion of which is returned to taxpayers in the form of subsidies or public investments.

1.6.2. *Tax reductions and the price signal*

Revenue raised by environmentally related taxation can be used to reduce marginal tax rates and distortions in other markets. A number of governments have implemented environmentally related taxation, particularly those taxes that impact on industry, in a revenue-neutral manner, *i.e.* revenues raised are fully recycled back to industry by some mechanism. For example, the Swedish NO_x charge is refunded back to industry in proportion to the polluters' energy production. However, revenue recycling can also be carried out in a revenue-positive or revenue-negative manner. In practice many governments that have introduced environmentally related taxes have reduced the marginal rates of distortionary taxes, in particular through cutting employers' social security contributions.

An advantage of revenue recycling is that it may alleviate sectoral competitiveness problems and thereby the pressure to grant business exemptions and rebates from environmentally related taxes (which the OECD/EU database on environmentally related taxes indicates are extensive). In this way higher, more environmentally effective tax rates can be implemented. However, revenue neutrality for industry as a whole does not necessarily mean revenue-neutrality for individual businesses, some firms will lose and some firms will gain, depending on the design of the tax and the recycling mechanism.

However, revenue recycling can distort price signals. Environmentally related taxes raise production costs and the market price of final goods. These price changes create economic signals that in the long run induce structural change in the economy, including incentives to use cleaner production technologies. Taxes also generate a second incentive effect, in that price increases tend to reduce demand for environmentally damaging products, and by altering relative prices create incentives for consumers to substitute towards cleaner goods, implying reduced production of polluting outputs. However, where revenues are recycled, these price signals may be muted or offset, depending on what taxes are reduced and by what means. For example, revenues may be recycled to industry in general, to the specific polluting industry or to fund research and development. If revenues are recycled to the polluting industries, and the recycling lowers tax-inclusive production costs in such a way that the initial impact of the environmental tax is cancelled out, then an optimal resource allocation, involving reduced production of the damaging products, may not result. Where revenues are recycled to industry, the key design criterion is to ensure that abatement incentives are not reduced, and more specifically that the amount of tax relief provided is not dependent on the environmental tax burden. In part because of the difficulty in recycling revenues to business while maintaining proper abatement incentives, in general most OECD countries have recycled revenue by reducing social security contributions across the economy as a whole, so that relative prices of cleaner goods fall and the output of polluting industries are reduced. Lump sum revenue recycling and grandfathered permits would also produce a full output effect.

1.7. The main obstacles to implementing environmentally related taxation

1.7.1. *Industrial competitiveness*

A key issue that has confronted countries which have implemented green tax reform, is the possible loss of international competitiveness of *some* economic sectors. The concept of "competitiveness" has several different levels. For instance, one should differentiate between the competitiveness of individual companies and sectors and the whole economy of a country. Environmentally related taxes raise the marginal costs of production for polluting firms. If firms decide not to relocate to countries without such taxes, then the most polluting firms will lose market share to less polluting firms. Alternatively firms could decide to relocate. Environmentally related tax exemptions and rebates are offered and/or revenues recycled to industry precisely to avoid the reduction in profitability of polluting industry and to prevent industry relocating. However, there are wider concepts of competitiveness, *i.e.* national and international competitiveness (see Box 2).

Competitiveness concerns are likely to be strongest if the polluting industry trades widely. Since the bulk of environmentally related taxes concern energy and transport taxes, the impact of such taxation will to a great extent vary between different sectors according to their energy intensity. Energy-intensive sectors would bear the burden of increased energy taxation whilst, if the revenue is recycled through reducing labour taxes, the competitiveness of labour-intensive production will improve. It is the reallocation of net taxation that creates conflicts of interests and opposition from those negatively affected by higher taxes. The impact on the economy overall will in part be determined by the relative weight of energy-intensive industries in the economy and the proportion of and the price elasticity of these sectors' exports. Koopmans (1998) for example estimates that the largely energy-intensive export industry in the Netherlands would be hard hit by energy taxes and that production losses in this sector are likely to exceed production gains in labour intensive sectors, at least in the short-run. However, Ekins and Speck (1998a) have shown that for the UK, where exports of energy-intensive production are

Box 2. **The concept of competitiveness**

It is important to distinguish clearly between the competitiveness of individual companies and sectors of the economy and that of the whole economy in general. Competitiveness will have a different meaning at each level. A *company* or *sector* is competitive if it is able to compete in international markets, with a satisfactory rate of return. For *a country as a whole*, the concept of competitiveness is more complex: at the economy-wide level, correcting for market failures provides an improvement in the overall economic outcome, and what represents increased costs for one firm or industry may lead to reduced costs for others.

One should also distinguish between a shorter and a longer time perspective. In the shorter run, exchange rate levels will be of importance. In the longer run, the country's ability to sustain a satisfactory wage level should also be taken into consideration. So also should its balance of payments and its ability to use its resources efficiently (including its labour resources). One definition of competitiveness, from the International Institute for Management Development (IIMD), is "the ability of a country to create added value and thus increase national wealth by managing assets and processes, attractiveness and aggressiveness, globality and proximity, and by integrating these relationships into an economic and social model" [IIMD (1996)]. When evaluating a particular policy, the effects on the economy are in general more important than the effects on certain individual sectors.

Source: OECD (1997).

relatively low, that the competitiveness of the economy as a whole is likely to improve with revenue neutral energy taxation.

Exemptions and rebates from environmentally related taxation are only one form of response to the competitiveness issue, where the design of such measures has a crucial impact on environmental effectiveness. There are other policy options that also reduce the negative impact on industrial competitiveness, but may retain more of the environmental effectiveness of the tax, for example, temporary relief, the use of complementary instruments, border tax adjustments (BTAs), and regional or international co-ordination of environmentally related taxation.

Some industry sectors (in particular energy intensive industries) are strongly opposed to environmentally related taxes on competitiveness grounds, specifically unilaterally introduced taxes, and therefore promote alternative policy instruments such as voluntary approaches [see OECD (1999a)]. Some countries, for example the UK and Denmark, have offered energy tax rebates to energy-intensive industry and firms on the condition that they meet negotiated energy efficiency agreements. Whether negotiated agreements improve the environmental effectiveness of a tax depends on two things: *i*) whether the full tax would have been imposed on the industry; *ii*) whether the negotiated agreements really produce environmental improvements significantly beyond what would have happened anyway.

Alternative policy instruments used to reduce environmental pollution, such as regulations and voluntary agreements, would also affect firm's costs and impact on the competitiveness position of individual sectors and the country as a whole. By enhancing the economic efficiency by which a given target is reached, properly designed environmentally related taxes will help minimise adverse effects on competitiveness nation-wide.

Border tax adjustments can reduce the competitiveness impacts of unilaterally imposed environmentally related taxation through the imposition of equivalent taxes on imported goods and the redemption of the environmentally related tax on exported goods. An example of a BTA in practice is that levied by the US on imported ozone depleting substances (ODS). The volume of ODS in imported product is estimated using US standard production data, however, countries that can prove that their products contain less ODS than these benchmarks are taxed at a lower rate. BTAs can be complicated to design and should be consistent with World Trade Organisation rules [see OECD (1996)].

Regionally or internationally co-ordinated environmentally related taxation would reduce arguments for exemptions and rebates based on international competitiveness. However, co-ordinated action does not mean that there will not be any winners or any losers. For example, a global tax on CO_2 emissions would be particularly costly for energy- and carbon-intensive economies (see Table 3).

1.7.2. *Income distribution concerns*

Taxes on production inputs are shifted onto higher prices, to lower wages, to lower rates of return on capital, or to lower resources prices.[6] Some environmentally related taxes are income regressive. That is, poorer households pay a disproportionate share of their income in these taxes relative to richer households. However, the *absolute impact* of a change in environmentally related taxation, for example a new energy tax, with revenues used to lower social security contribution, on household disposable income would be the net effect of several different elements:

1. the increased burden resulting from the *tax increases*;
2. the *compensation* effect resulting from lower social security contributions;
3. the repercussions of the various tax *exemptions*;
4. the *induced effects* of any employment changes; and
5. the distribution of the *environmental benefits* resulting from the tax.[7]

Equity concerns can be an obstacle to environmentally related taxation and therefore governments often design taxes with various mitigation and compensation measures, *i.e.* items (2) and (3) above.

The OECD definitions of mitigation and compensation are as follows [OECD (1994)]:

"Mitigation refers to reducing the impacts of the programme *ex ante* so that the potential impacts do not occur." An example of a mitigation measure is to establish a consumption tax floor below which no tax is levied in order to protect low-income (small) users. "Compensation refers to aid to particular groups *ex post* so that they are (at least partly) 'made whole'."

Compensation measures are corrective measures, such as lump sum compensation, calculated on the basis of average tax payments per household.[8] *Tax shifting*,[9] *i.e.* the reduction of other taxes, such as labour and income taxes (see Section 2.3) is a widespread form of compensation. The regressive impact of an environmentally related tax will be (partially) compensated by a reduction in the marginal rates of other taxes, specifically taxes on labour. The net distributional implication of this approach is, however, not clear: the offsetting mechanisms can themselves be income regressive. For example, cuts in income taxation may not benefit many low-income households, because they pay little or no income taxes [Smith (1998)].

Mitigation measures reduce the environmental effectiveness of the tax by cancelling out some of the incentives to change consumption and investment behaviour. Compensation measures could be improved if they were targeted at low-income groups and other factors that cause the equity problem. For example, although low income is a factor that influences energy efficiency in households, there are other factors, for example tenure (renting not owning) and lack of capital to invest in more energy efficient heating and electrical equipment.[10] Therefore, where the root cause is not low income, other policies, for example direct regulations and subsidies, might be more environmentally effective than mitigation and compensation measures.[11]

The outcome, in terms of environmental improvement (including health benefits, property price rises, higher standard of living, etc.),[12] will also be unevenly distributed across different groups. Where environmental pressures are distributed in a regressive manner, with low income households being exposed to higher risks, this does not imply that pollution reduction will automatically lead to a progressive distribution of the protection benefits. Richer households may benefit more than poorer households may, particularly if the benefits are measured in monetary terms, since their willingness to pay for improvements will be higher than for low-income households. Protection measures could even negatively affect low-income groups. For example, in Germany traditional measures aimed at reductions in local air pollution loads have led to a wider dissemination of pollutants, causing problems of soil acidification and forest damage in rural regions, far away from the sources of industrial pollution. However, in many instances low-income households live in particularly polluted areas, for example congested inner cities, and therefore these same household s may experience the greatest environmental improvement and benefits following the implementation of an environmentally effective tax.

In assessing the impact of a tax on low-income groups it is important to calculate the overall impact of the tax reform, including the impact of any mitigation measures and compensation payments, and any (employment) effects resulting from revenue recycling measures.

1.8. Environmentally related taxation in policy mixes

Taxation is one policy instrument available for environmental protection. Other policy instruments are non-auctioned or auctioned tradable emission permits, voluntary negotiated agreements, deposit-refund schemes, subsidies, and traditional command and control measures. While there are some examples of emission trading schemes in the USA, there are few in Europe. Smith [in OECD (1999d)] identifies three problems of compatibility between a mix of instruments applied to the same problem. Policy mixes can be:

- *inefficient* (if keeping an inflexible instrument in place prevents the efficient reallocation of abatement efforts);
- *unnecessary* (if only one instrument actually is effective); and thus
- *wasteful* (if using more than one instrument leads to additional administrative costs to be borne either by the government or the regulated emitters).

Schreiner [in OECD (1999d)] is only in favour of combining measures if the various measures *supplement* each other in a predictable way to achieve a desired outcome, and if a single policy instrument could not achieve the same outcome more effectively. He argues that the efficiency of the main economic instrument is undermined by the addition of overlapping, not supplementary, policies. Multiple instruments may raise costs, because each instrument is likely to have separate administrative requirements, and be regulated by a different government department. Compliance costs for the polluters are also likely to be higher with the increased complexity of regulatory arrangements.

In practice taxes, voluntary agreements and regulations are often used in policy mixes, but there are few examples of the theoretically interesting combination of taxes and trading (see Section 2.4 for further discussion of the advantages and disadvantages of policy combinations).

NOTES

1. This section is based on OECD (1996).

2. A more complete and practical assessment of the implications of introducing an environmental tax (*e.g.*, energy tax) would address distributional effects (across different households and firms), technological substitution options, measurement difficulties and administrative costs.

3. The marginal benefit (MB) from polluting an additional unit – or alternatively, the marginal abatement cost (including technology costs and reduced profits) incurred when restricting pollution by an additional unit – is assumed to be low at high pollution levels, and then increase as pollution is restricted (moving along the horizontal axis, from right to left). Private pollution costs (captured by MC) could be zero or positive (as shown in Figure 1) and tied to disposal/clean-up costs. Where private pollution costs are zero, the marginal social cost (MSC) schedule would coincide with the marginal environmental cost (MEC) schedule, with the private market (pre-tax) equilibrium established where the MB schedule intersects the horizontal axis.

4. This section is based on Barde (2000).

5. While it is true that the original rates of landfill tax were based on research into external costs, the rates have since been increased, in order to help secure a given environmental target: the requirements of the European Union's landfill directive and the National Waste Strategy.

6. The distributional impact of a tax is related to the incidence of a tax. The final incidence of a tax depends on the relative demand and supply elasticities for the taxed good. For instance, the buyer will bear most of the tax if demand for the good is firm despite the tax and production can easily be increased or decreased, for example automotive fuels. However, the seller will bear most of the tax if supply is difficult to vary and demand responds strongly downwards to higher prices, for example some chlorinated solvents. The burden of taxation on the seller will in turn be shared between capital, labour, and resource owners.

7. See Christiansen and Tietenberg (1985) for a survey of US empirical studies on the distribution of benefits of environmental policies.

8. Although lump sum transfers can alleviate the burden of increased taxation it would be difficult (and not necessarily desirable, in terms of incentives) to exactly compensate income losses as households with similar incomes use different amounts of energy and pay different amounts of related taxes.

9. By tax shifting, it is here meant shifting taxes to pollution from other distortionary taxation, not the shifting of the tax burden. The extent to which the burden of a tax, for example a petrol tax levied on producers, can be shifted to the end user, is determined by the demand price elasticity.

10. See Brechling and Smith (1994).

11. For example, direct subsidies could be offered to pensioners, other low-income tax paying households and to social housing for energy-efficiency investments. Alternatively, legislation could provide incentives for landlords to invest in the energy efficiency of their rented accommodation, including heating systems, etc.

12. Although there are tools to measure these benefits, including hedonic pricing and willingness to pay surveys, it can be difficult/controversial to estimate such benefits. Despite these difficulties, an attempt to calculate these benefits should be included in an assessment of the impact of environmentally related taxes on the distribution of household income.

Chapter 2

OPTIONS FOR GREEN TAX REFORM

2.1. The background to green tax reform

Various fiscal policies can affect the environment. Environmentally related taxes can impact on the environment by reducing pollution, waste and resource depletion, but other taxes, tax expenditures, and subsidies also impact on the environment. For instance, special tax relief given to certain polluting activities, reduced tax levels for certain fuels (*e.g.* diesel), outright tax exemptions for aviation kerosene, tax deductibility of car commuting expenses and certain kinds of subsidies (*e.g.* on coal) can all work against environmental policy objectives. The impact of government intervention on the environment should therefore be considered in the context of comprehensive reforms of the tax and subsidy systems. Such reforms are sometimes referred to as "green tax reforms".

The wider background for green tax reform has been a political initiative in many countries to introduce greater flexibility and efficiency into their economic structures. In the last 15 years significant tax reform has been undertaken in most OECD countries. This has resulted in sizeable reductions in tax rates in the higher-income tax brackets (which fell on average by more than 10% between 1986 and 1997) and a lowering of corporate tax rates (around 10% over the same period). In addition, tax-bases have been broadened, and there has been an increase in the role of general consumption taxes, such as VAT. This thorough overhaul of tax systems has provided an opportunity to increase the use of environmentally related taxation.

2.2. Targets of green tax reform

The main options for green tax reform open to policymakers consists of three complementary policies: the removal of subsidies, the restructuring of existing taxes so as not to encourage polluting activities and introducing new environmentally related taxes. Revenues from such reforms can then, for example, be used to cut marginal tax rates of other distortionary taxation in the economy, in order to achieve a so-called "double dividend". Bosquet (2000) identifies two other possible revenue streams: taxes on resource use and on resource rents (excess profits).

2.2.1. *Reducing environmentally harmful tax expenditures*

Governments have historically manipulated prices in the market through regulations, tax policies, government ownership, subsidised loans, purchase commitments, budgetary transfers, trade barriers, and price setting in order to enhance the competitiveness of certain products, processes, activities, industries, social groups, or regions. Most interventions are either paid for through government budgets, or reduce the receipts financing these budgets. However, there also exists a number of off-budget support measures, including market price support,[1] low rate-of-return requirements, and exemptions from environmental standards. The non-internalisation of social and environmental externalities can also be classified as a subsidy, in that it allows insufficient provision for future environmental liabilities. Furthermore, there are many regulations, which are not obvious support measures, but can serve the same purpose (*e.g.* restrictions on third party access to electricity distribution networks).

Although data on support levels is not comprehensive, fairly reliable data for agriculture, fisheries, industry, and coal support are presented in Table 1. The data shows that support levels have fluctuated and that only for coal has there been a clear downward trend in overall support.[2]

Table 1. **Support levels in OECD countries**
US$ billion

	1987	1989	1990	1991	1992	1993	1994	1995	1996	1997	1998
Agriculture	326				394					336p	362p
Marine capture fisheries									6.8	6.3	
Coal production	13.2			10.8	11.9	9.0	10.3	11.0	9.3	7.7	6.1p
Industry		36.9	41.6	45.7	44.1	43.7					

Notes: p = preliminary. *Agriculture*: total support estimate for agriculture; data for 1987 represents an average for 1986-88, for 1992 an average of 1991-1993. *Fisheries*: government financial transfers to marine capture fisheries. *Coal production*: producer support equivalent in selected OECD countries (Germany, Japan, Spain, Turkey, UK). *Industry*: reported net government expenditures to industry. Note that the support to industry overlaps with other support estimates, *e.g.* to energy.
Source: OECD (1998), OECD (1999c), OECD (2000d) and IEA (199a).

Over the last two decades, many OECD countries have reduced or eliminated direct energy subsidies and lifted price controls, as part of a general move away from heavy government intervention in energy markets and towards market deregulation. As part of this process, the levels of support to coal producers in selected OECD countries has been declining, sometimes significantly. Thus, the UK,[3] Belgium and Portugal all removed their coal production support in the last decade [IEA (1999b)]. These reductions in support to coal production have been accompanied by decreases in the total production of coal in these countries; often coinciding with a substitution towards less polluting fuels, such as natural gas, especially in electricity generation. New subsidies have, however, been introduced to promote more benign and renewable energy sources and technologies, and subsidies to traditional fuel sources are being geared towards developing cleaner processes, greater energy use efficiency, and reducing emissions [IEA (1999a)].

The second category of distortion arises from tax measures. Tax rate variations between substitute goods can influence market structure. For example, diesel fuel is taxed at a lower rate than petrol in most OECD countries, although diesel vehicles are more polluting compared to their petrol counterparts.[4] This tax differential has been a factor contributing to the large increase in the number of diesel vehicles on the road: in OECD countries, the consumption of diesel fuel for road transport grew from 15% of total road fuel consumption in 1970 to 32% in 1997 [OECD (1999a)]. In addition, special tax incentives (*e.g.*, accelerated depreciation, resource allowances, flow-through share provisions) given to certain industries, for example to mining and forestry industries, can be harmful to the environment.

There are many more examples of current tax expenditure/subsidies in OECD countries that damage the environment. Therefore, a starting point of green tax reform should be to undertake a systematic correction of subsidies and taxes which on balance are harmful to the environment and evidence of government intervention failure. Recent experiences in OECD countries indicate that the reform or removal of many of these subsidies may not only increase economic efficiency and reduce the burden on government budgets and consumers, but can also alleviate environmental pressures – resulting in so-called "win-win-win" benefits. Box 3 highlights some recent attempts to quantify the benefits of subsidy removal.

2.2.2. *Restructuring existing environmentally related taxes*

Many existing environmentally related taxes could be modified so as to benefit the environment (*e.g.*, fully internalise the external costs of the activity), while balancing other policy objectives.[5] An example would be the restructuring of the base of energy taxes (implicit carbon taxes) to more closely

---

Box 3. **Effects of energy support removal**

A number of OECD studies have simulated the effects of removing coal and other energy subsidies, either at the world level or the country level. All the studies found significant *environmental* benefits from subsidy removal in terms of reductions in CO_2 emissions, with CO_2 emissions from the sectors concerned declining by between 1-8% in 2010 compared with the base case (OECD, 1997c). Where the effects on the *economy* were analysed, most of the studies estimated real increases in gross domestic or gross national product. As would be expected, some of the studies also found significant reductions in *employment* in the coal sector from reduced coal production, by as much as 104 000 mining jobs in Europe and Japan (DRI, 1997).

---

reflect the carbon-content of different fuels. Carbon taxes would create direct incentives for reducing carbon emissions. The environmental impact of tax restructuring is determined by the total tax pattern, in this example, the whole pattern of taxes across different fuels and the relative prices of substitute products and activities.

Environmentally motivated differentiation of diesel taxes is applied in Austria, Denmark, Finland, Norway, Sweden and the UK. Finland, Denmark, Norway and Sweden apply differentiated taxes on unleaded gasoline, according to environmental criteria (*e.g.* in Sweden according to the sulphur, benzene and phosphorous content of automotive fuels). This type of tax rate differentiation has lead to a gradual reduction in the use of the most polluting automotive fuels. Several countries (*e.g.* Austria, Denmark, Germany, and Norway) have introduced differentiated vehicle taxation adjusted to the specific emission characteristics of the vehicles, whilst the US levies a tax on "gas guzzlers". (See Sections 3.2 and 3.3 for more information.)

2.2.3. *Introducing new environmentally related taxes*[6]

Another option for green tax reform is to introduce new taxes, either on *emissions* or *products*, principally to protect the environment. Emissions to air, land, and water are often still regulated by direct controls not emission taxes, however, in the last decade, new taxes have been introduced on products ranging from packaging to fertilisers, pesticides, batteries, chemical substances (*e.g.* solvents), lubricants, tyres, razors and disposable cameras. The OECD/EU database on environmentally related taxes records a large number of taxes on such tax-bases.

The database is an interesting tool not only for highlighting the huge range of taxes levied – and the exemptions and rebates – but also for highlighting what is omitted. Although, all OECD countries levy taxation on some types of energy products, in most countries, coal and heavy fuel oils used in industry, and aviation fuel used on international flights, are not taxed, even though the consumption of these fossil fuels causes both CO_2 emissions and other types of pollution. This effectively means that a large proportion of total carbon emissions in OECD countries is untaxed. The outcome is that the current pattern of carbon emission reduction is far from optimal because many low-cost abatement options are exempted from taxation. Products and polluters currently exempted from taxation could be targets for new taxation.

2.3. Double dividend possibilities

The term "double dividend" refers to the possibility that a revenue neutral environmentally related tax shift could generate two possible benefits or dividends. The first dividend is in terms of more effective environmental protection[7] (gains from the static and dynamic efficiency of environmentally related taxes), while the second dividend arises from the reduction in other distortionary taxes. Depending on which marginal tax rates are cut and the specific country considered,

---

the second dividend could generate employment gains, investment gains and/or a more efficient economy.

The reason why shifting taxation to pollution from labour and capital taxes can result in a double dividend is because the raising of tax revenues causes departures between the marginal social benefits and the marginal social costs of taxed activities, thereby imposing efficiency or "welfare" costs on the economy (see Box 4). Environmentally related taxation also carries a tax burden and it is the interaction between this burden and other distortionary taxes in the economy that determines whether or not a double dividend can be realised.

Box 4. **Efficiency costs tied to taxation**

Pigou (1947) pointed out that the financing of public expenditure by distortionary taxes imposes an efficiency loss on the economy, *i.e.* the marginal cost of public funds (MCF) will be greater than one for each unit raised. Therefore, this efficiency loss should be included when undertaking a cost-benefit analysis of public expenditure, *i.e.* the MCF raises costs. Sandmo (1998) explains that the "although the tax system as a whole is distortionary, some elements of it are less distortionary than others. If an increase in the supply of public goods is financed on the margin by an increase of the less distortionary parts of the system, the marginal cost of funds might well be less than one."

Ballard and Medema (1993) calculate the efficiency effects of different taxes using US data. In the same study they also calculate the relative efficiency of pollution taxes and pollution subsidies. In their model subsidies are financed by an increase in distortionary taxes whilst the revenues raised by pollution taxes are used to offset other distortionary taxation. The results show that pollution taxes are significantly more efficient than pollution subsidies.

The double dividend literature however casts doubt on whether in each instance a double dividend will result from a shift away from labour (or capital) taxation in favour of environmental taxation. For example, with nominal wage rigidities, the introduction of an environmental tax that raises production costs and general price levels (and thus lowers real wages) can have a negative employment effects that offsets positive employment effects stemming from a personal income or payroll tax reduction. Also, environmentally related taxes are specific taxes, often with a narrow base, and a large excess burden because of the interaction with other taxation. This excess burden results because environmentally related taxes raise consumer prices, reduce real wages, reduce the labour supply and labour taxation revenues, and therefore other taxation has to be increased to maintain total revenues.

The net welfare impact of revenue-neutrally shifting taxes from labour or capital to pollution may be broken down into three components:

a) a *primary welfare gain* that results from the environmental benefits of the reform, net of the reduction in consumer surplus from higher pollution prices;

b) a *revenue-recycling effect*, or efficiency gain, that is positive when the revenue raised by the environmentally related tax is recycled *via* cuts in distortionary taxation; and

c) a *tax interaction effect*, that has three components, as per Parry *et al.* (1999). The first component is the efficiency loss from the reduction in labour supply in response to higher pollution prices that reduce real wages. The second and third components are the requirements to raise additional tax revenue on other factors of production (capital in particular) to replace the revenue lost from the reduction in labour taxes and to keep real government spending constant in the face of higher prices. The tax interaction effect has a negative welfare impact, as the burden of the environmentally related tax is partly shifted onto other factors of production, intensifying the efficiency losses of pre-existing tax distortions.

Additionally, dynamic efficiency gains may be realised given ongoing incentives for further emissions reductions to avoid environmental taxes on existing emissions levels, through industrial restructuring and the search for cost-efficient abatement technologies and procedures.

In terms of the above analysis, the existence of a double dividend depends on the relative size of the revenue recycling and tax interaction effects. It should also be noted that it is difficult in practice to determine the tax rate reduction on a given base (*e.g.*, income, payroll) that will give rise to a revenue neutral outcome, either on a current or present value basis, given uncertainty over behavioural responses to tax changes (*i.e.*, the elasticity of each tax-base with respect to its tax rate) in the short and long run. These various considerations over the interaction between an environmentally related tax and existing distortionary taxes means that a double environment-employment dividend does not follow automatically from a given "green tax reform".

2.3.1. Realising a double dividend

The theoretical and empirical evidence for a double dividend is not conclusive, nevertheless, a number of governments are implementing revenue-neutral green tax reform with the explicit intention of realising some double dividend. If it could be demonstrated that positive employment effects follow from switching the burden of taxation to pollution from labour, this evidence could counterbalance the competitiveness and equity arguments used against implementing new or higher environmentally related taxes. A key question for many governments intent on introducing or raising rates on environmentally related taxes is the reliability of the double dividend and how to realise it. Without being exhaustive, a number of key conditions for the realisation of a double dividend can be mentioned here.[8]

- *The initial structure of the tax system* is sub-optimal, in order for a dividend to emerge from removing sub-optimal tax provisions.

- The *tax incidence* is a crucial issue. If the burden of pollution taxes finally falls upon consumers through higher prices of the taxed commodities, the reduction of the tax wedge on labour will be less effective, and the employment effect reduced, or eliminated. Since labour is a relatively immobile factor of production, this ultimate tax incidence on labour is likely to occur.

- The degree of *substitutability between factors of production* is important: if it is possible to use more labour instead of energy and capital, increased employment is more likely to occur.

- The issue of the *mobility of production factors* is crucial. In the case of an energy tax, if labour is a better substitute for energy than capital, there will be a shift to more labour-intensive production techniques. If capital is relatively immobile internationally, the tax burden will be shifted to capital. If, however, capital is internationally mobile, it could move abroad to avoid the tax. For this reason a double dividend is less likely to occur in a small open economy than in a larger economy.

- A double dividend tends to be found more frequently in models with *wage rigidities*. If wages are rigid, then a cut in social security contributions will reduce labour costs and employers will hire more labour. In contrast, if wages were flexible, the resulting higher employment would bid up real wages, cancelling out employment gains.

- The *environmental effectiveness* of the tax: the more effective the environmentally related tax is, the more rapidly the tax base will erode. Therefore, to maintain the same revenue flow, governments will have to increase other taxes, or increase existing environmentally related taxes with two possible consequences: a further tax incidence on labour, or a possible reduction in pollution beyond the optimal level. In this case, environmentally related taxes would exacerbate tax distortions.

2.3.2. Empirical evidence for a double dividend

To test the double dividend hypothesis some economists have simulated such tax shifts using macro economic models. Majocchi's (1996) survey of the evidence on the double dividend has shown that the results of many models converge, to indicate that a carbon-energy tax combined with cuts in labour taxation, would yield some double employment-environment dividend. However, the employment effect is limited; with many models calculating a small increase in employment. More recent simulations show similar results: a real, but small potential for a double dividend [OECD (2000c)]. The main conclusions are summarised in Box 5.

Box 5.   **Main conclusions from existing studies on the double dividend**

In general, a tax shift from the relative abundant factor labour to the scarce factor environment leads to positive effects on employment (*substitution effect*) and negative effects on GDP (*nominal income effect*). Theoretical studies show that negative employment effects can be expected if the negative income effects of the tax dominate the substitution effect due to the change in the relative factor input prices. However, simulation studies, based on traditional assumptions with regard to substitution elasticities, show a dominance of the substitution effect.

Positive employment effects can be expected if the revenues are used to reduce *labour taxation* in general and employer/employee social security contributions in particular. In contrast, if the revenue is used for lump sum payments to households or to lower VAT, it leads to less significant or negative employment effects.

For most European countries, larger employment effects can be expected if the cut in social security contributions are targeted at the *unskilled labour* force.

E*armarking* of a large proportion of the revenues raised, for instance for environmental investment, reduces the potential double dividend benefit.

Positive effects on GDP can be expected if the revenues are used to cut *capital taxes*, (thus favouring investment), and if the environmentally related taxes are gradually implemented.

Both GDP and employment effects depend on the *size of tax shifts*. A significant benefit would require substantial cuts in labour taxation and therefore broad tax bases for environmentally related taxes would be required, for instance taxes on energy or transport. Generally, the results of the simulations show positive effects on GDP and employment when the energy tax is introduced stepwise and the energy price increase does not exceed 4% to 5% per year.

The effects in the labour market are larger if unemployment is linked with *wage rigidity*: if the real wage level does not decrease with unemployment, lower social security contributions are more likely to induce positive employment effects.

Negative impacts on *international competitiveness* can be controlled effectively by introducing offsetting methods, such as border tax adjustments, sectoral recycling of the revenue or a rebate scheme for buffering the negative short term effects on energy intensive industries.

Source: Based on OECD (2000c).

Another survey, Bosquet (2000), examined the evidence for a double dividend from 139 simulations[9] of the impacts of carbon/energy tax shifts in 56 countries. Energy taxes reduced carbon emissions in just 84% of the simulations. Concerning a second dividend, 73% of the simulations predicted that employment would rise. The mode of recycling revenues matters significantly. Cuts in social security contributions produced higher employment than cuts in personal income tax. The time horizon was also found to be significant, with long-term simulations more likely to predict negative employment impacts than short- or medium-term simulations.

Bosquet (2000) also tested for evidence of increased economic activity following a tax shift. There is some debate whether GDP, the measure used, is appropriate, as it does not incorporate "welfare" values – it has been argued that environmental improvement may come at the expense of GDP. 51% of the simulations predicted reductions in GDP following the implementation of carbon/energy taxation.

The mode of recycling revenues is significant: 65% of simulations that cut social security contributions resulted in increased GDP, compared to just 23% when personal income tax was cut. Furthermore, time also matters: long-term simulations more often predicted reductions in GDP than short- or medium-term simulations. 77% of the simulations predicted that investment would decline following green tax reform, resulting from a substitution effect against capital and negative demand effects in the polluting sectors. Finally, 94% of the simulations predicted a rise in the consumer price index, illustrating the limited capacity of the economy to substitute away from carbon intensive processes and products.

2.3.3. *The reliability of the empirical evidence*

Bosquet (2000) lists a number of potential problems with the models used in many simulation studies. The simulations are based on *ex ante* modelling and it is difficult to test their performance *ex post*, because of the complexity of the interactions between environmentally related taxation, revenue recycling and employment, investment, prices, and GDP. Most models omit a factor for structural unemployment. It is likely that some structural unemployment is due to wage rigidities, and by excluding this factor the models underestimate employment improvement, following cuts in social security contributions, that improve labour market flexibility. The simulations thus incorporate a large degree of uncertainty.

2.3.4. *Double dividend policies in practice*

Although the available theoretical and empirical results do not indicate clearly that a double dividend can be realised, Sweden, Denmark, the Netherlands, the United Kingdom, Finland, Norway, Germany, and Italy have implemented green tax reforms, and recycled the revenue in a way that may produce some double dividend. In Finland and Sweden, and to some extent in Germany, green tax reform has occurred in a revenue-negative manner, *i.e.* the overall tax burden has declined. In the other countries, strict revenue-neutrality has been followed, *i.e.* the tax burden has remained constant. Some governments have plans for more environmental tax reform packages, *i.e.* the UK's tax on industry and business use of energy (2001) and on the extraction of mineral aggregates (2002). Other governments are considering such tax shifts, for example in France, the revenue from new industrial energy tax will be entirely allocated to a reduction in employers' social security contributions, for those enterprises implementing the new legislation, limiting work to 35 hours per week. Table 2 shows the double dividend packages followed in these eight countries.

The table shows that:

- tax shifting is a recent policy, with Sweden as the pioneer;

- tax shifts undertaken have been relatively small, except in Sweden and Denmark;

- environmentally related taxes are raised on emissions from the burning of fossil fuels and landfill waste disposal – these pollutants are relatively inelastically demanded and therefore raise large relatively stable revenues necessary to fund equivalent cuts in labour taxation; and

- tax cuts have focused on labour taxes and more recently employers' social security contributions, *i.e.* to realise the double environment employment dividend.

2.3.5. *Double dividend policy issues*

There are two main policy issues with double dividend policies. First, the realisation of the double dividend is uncertain. Second, although, independently, both elements of the tax reform point in the right direction: lowering labour costs and improving the environment (and the efficiency of environmental policy), a strict revenue linkage may turn out to be disadvantageous in the longer run. It is unclear what action a government would take to secure funding for the associated reductions in labour taxation, if the tax policy is more environmentally effective than anticipated and consequently tax revenues are less than expected. More *ex post* assessment of double dividend policy packages is needed.

Table 2. **Double dividend packages**

	Start year	Taxes raised on	Tax cut	Magnitude
Sweden	1990	CO_2 SO_2 Various	PIT Energy taxes on agriculture Continuous education	2.4% of total tax revenue
Denmark	1994	Various[1] CO_2 SO_2	PIT SSC Capital income	Around 3% of GDP by 2002, or over 6% of total tax revenue
Netherlands	1996	CO_2	CPT, PIT, SSC	0.3% of GDP in 1996, or around 0.5% of total tax revenue
United Kingdom	1996	Landfill	SSC	Around 0.1% of total tax revenues in 1999
Norway	1999	CO_2 SO_2 Diesel Oil	PIT	0.2% of total tax revenue in 1999
Germany	1999	Petroleum products	SSC	Around 1% of total tax revenue in 1999
Italy	1999	Petroleum products	SSC	Less than 0.1% of total tax revenue in 1999

1. (Gasoline, electricity, water, waste, cars.) PIT is personal income tax, CPT is corporation tax, SSC is social security contributions. In 1996, the Netherlands introduced a CO_2 tax and made cuts to personal and corporate income tax, and social security contributions largely to increase public acceptability of the environmental tax (rather than to address market inefficiencies per se in the labour and capital (savings) markets)
Source: Bosquet (2000).

2.4. Policy packages

Economic instruments are rarely single-policy instruments in the context of environmental protection programmes. The possibility of combining environmentally related taxes with tradable permits and voluntary agreements, although a challenge to industry and government could provide added flexibility, environmental certainty, and reduced costs. However, poorly designed policy packages could obscure incentives and generate wasteful overlap.

2.4.1. *Environmentally related taxation and regulation*

A frequent policy mix is environmentally related taxation combined with regulation. For instance, in waste policy governments may levy a wastewater tax and have regulations on wastewater discharges from industry, or a combination of landfill taxation with regulations on packaging waste and recycling targets. In energy policy, a number of governments set relatively low rates in energy/carbon taxes, supplemented with command and control energy efficiency requirements, and sector-wide best available technology regulations and energy efficiency labelling for consumer white goods. Concerning local/regional air pollution, governments combine taxation on SO_2 with regulations on sulphur-content in fuels, and technology standards for power stations (*e.g.* flue gas desulphurisation). In transport policy, governments combine taxation of vehicles and automotive fuels, with fuel and fuel efficiency standards, weight limits on heavy vehicles, and speed limits.

Environmental policy was originally largely based on command and control regulations. In many cases governments have implemented environmentally related taxation without first removing regulations, even though the regulatory incentives maybe effectively and more efficiently replaced by taxes. In fact, in many OECD countries the reform of government regulations is high on the political agenda. The objective is not necessarily to "deregulate", but to make government interventions more efficient, thereby reducing the cost imposed on the regulated sectors and improving the environmental effectiveness of environmental policy. The choice of environmental policy instrument in this reform process is key. Governments may implement environmentally related taxes, and add regulations to supplement the tax incentive, in situations where competitiveness or distribution concerns limit the use of revenue raising instruments, or where taxes for other reasons are constrained to very low levels. In both cases, where regulation overlaps rather than supplements the incentives created by the taxes – the most environmentally and cost effective instruments should be chosen.

2.4.2. *Environmentally related taxation and voluntary approaches*

A recent OECD assessment of the performance of voluntary approaches [see OECD (1999a)] recorded the widespread use in OECD countries of voluntary approaches, which are generally regarded as inferior to environmental taxes in addressing environmental objectives. A large number of these approaches have been surveyed: over 300 negotiated agreements in European Union countries, about 30 000 local pollution control agreements in Japan and over 40 public voluntary programmes managed by the US government at the federal level. Voluntary approaches are favoured by industry for the flexibility they embody and as a means to avoid other regulation or taxation. Governments may also see voluntary agreements as offering practical advantages in terms of implementation. However, voluntary approaches are fraught with a number of potential pitfalls, as identified in Box 6. The 1999 report identifies problems with voluntary approaches, and offers a number of "guidelines" to improve both management and performance.

Some governments have combined negotiated agreements concerning energy efficiency with either carbon or energy taxes. In Denmark, concessions on the CO_2 tax have been granted to industries on the condition that they enter a negotiated agreement with the government to increase energy efficiency. The forthcoming UK tax on industry and business use of energy similarly offers an 80% discount, for energy intensive sectors that sign energy efficiency agreements with the government. However, while a negotiated agreement might improve an industry's energy efficiency (if the agreement is tough enough), it does nothing to switch demand away from energy-intensive industries, which is one of the beneficial effects of energy taxes.

Box 6. The pitfalls of voluntary approaches

Voluntary approaches have several weaknesses and should be designed and implemented to avoid a number of pitfalls:

- *Weak control*: either because industry does not provide adequate control mechanisms, or because of a lack of sanctions.
- *"Free-riding"*: if the agreement does not contain monitoring and sanctions there is a risk that parties will not comply with it, thus avoiding the costs of pollution abatement.
- *Transaction costs*: if the number of stakeholders is high, the cost of negotiation and of setting up the agreement may be high.
- *Regulatory capture*: there is a risk that powerful and well organised industry organisations may "capture' the policy and regulatory process by avoiding or obstructing the introduction of a regulation and/or influencing the regulatory process to their own benefit, and to the detriment of other parts of society. A typical consequence is a "business as usual scenario" in which the agreement does not in fact result in any additional action or environmental benefit, as the environmental protection measures taken are those which would have occurred anyway.
- *Loss of revenue* compared to a tax alternative, with associated "excess burden" implications (see Section 2.3).

Source: OECD (1999a).

Negotiated agreements have also been concluded in non-energy sectors. For example, in Belgium the battery industry signed an agreement on recycling rates for batteries with federal and regional governments. The battery industry is responsible for collecting and recycling used batteries sold in Belgium. The agreement specifies certain collection targets that the battery industry must fulfil: 40% in 1996 rising to 67.5% in 1999 and 75% in 2000. The batteries collected must be recycled according to the agreements signed with the regional governments. In return for meeting this agreement, batteries collected by the voluntary collection scheme are not subject to the "ecotax" levied on batteries.

Despite a number of success stories,[10] the OECD report on voluntary approaches concludes that there is limited evidence as to their environmental effectiveness. Marginal abatement costs will tend to differ substantially between firms within a negotiated agreement, and without some other mechanism, for example trading, no incentive exist to exploit these differences for cost-effective abatement. The report also concludes that administrative costs and transaction costs associated with negotiated agreements are often high. Negotiated agreements produce no price signal and therefore create no incentive for cost minimisation, or for consumers to change their purchasing patterns (see Section 1.6.2). Negotiated agreements provide little incentive for industry to innovate (see Section 1.4), whereas taxes provide dynamic incentives for abatement and production innovation. For all these reasons, the use of voluntary approaches in environmental policy should be carefully assessed.

2.4.3. *Environmentally related taxes and emission/pollution trading*

In theory environmentally related taxes and tradable permits can be complementary instruments in both domestic and international policy. However, there is currently only one example of such a policy mix, namely for CFCs in the US (see Box 7), although UK waste policy combines taxes on landfilled waste and trading of Packaging Waste Recovery Notes (annual producer waste minimisation obligations). In spite of the lack of experience in such policy combinations, a number of countries, including Germany and the United Kingdom, have proposals to combine domestic energy/carbon taxation and domestic carbon-equivalent emission trading in advance of an anticipated international emission trading system.[11]

The OECD is developing guidelines for domestic transferable permit systems for environmental policy. An argument for combining taxes and emissions trading is that the transaction costs of emissions trading, in term of measuring and monitoring emissions, may be too high for some sectors, in terms of the verification and certification of emissions reduction. In such circumstances, the government could offer such sectors, for example small businesses, the option to pay a carbon/energy tax instead. The tax in effect is a price cap for sectors outside the trading scheme. In this case the emissions trading scheme would be restricted to the small number of large, point source emitters, for example, electricity generators and energy-intensive industry. Another situation in which a government might introduce this policy combination is to supplement a (grandfathered) permit system with taxes to both raise revenues, and to reduce incentives to stock permits, in order to maintain the fluidity of the market (*e.g.* the US ODC tax). A final situation is the possibility to combine internationally traded permits with domestic taxes. The facility to trade internationally reduces the need for domestic abatement and the permit system also creates added certainty that "targets' can be met. The Japanese study described below is an example of such a system.

A recent Japanese study [EIEP (2000)] concluded that a combination of a carbon tax and emissions trading would reduce the economic cost of cutting CO_2 emissions, compared to a pure carbon tax policy. The pure carbon tax policy is their baseline case. The study models the tax rates necessary to achieve a 2% cut in CO_2 emissions by 2010 from 1990 levels. Simulations show that a baseline carbon tax of between $273 and $364 per tonne of carbon would be necessary. The policy mix assumed an upper limit for international emission purchases of 25% of the total 2% emission reduction modelled. This represented 15 million tonnes of carbon bought at an estimated price of $91 per tonne of carbon.[12] The associated carbon tax required to meet the residual emission reduction, was calculated at a lower $241 per tonne of carbon. This policy combination was predicted to reduce GDP in 2010 by 0.1%, compared to a 0.2-0.7% contraction under the pure carbon tax policy. Even though Japan currently

> ### Box 7. Ozone depleting chemical taxation and quota trading in the US
>
> The US government levies taxes on ODCs according to their ozone depletion potential. For example, a pound of CFC-11 is taxed $7.60, compared to a pound of halon-1301 at $76.00 (see Annex III, Table 1, for a full list of the tax rates). A number of exemptions apply: ODCs used in metered-dose inhalers, recycled ODCs, and ODCs used as feedstock. A credit on the tax paid is refunded for these exceptions. The taxes are levied on ODC manufacturers and importers. The US government applies Border Tax Adjustments to these taxes, *i.e.* exported products are refunded the tax and imported products containing ODCs, or – perhaps more interestingly – where ODCs are believed to have been used in the production process, are taxed. The ODC weight is calculated either by a standard method or based on exact measurement, if this can be proven. If the weight of ODC used in a product is difficult to determine, then the tax is calculated by a value method, equivalent to 1% of the entry value of the product.
>
> In addition to these ODC taxes on production and imports a tax on floor stocks is also levied if stocks of:
>
> 1. at least 400 pounds of ODCs (excluding items 2 and 3);
> 2. at least 50 pounds of halons; or
> 3. at least 1 000 pounds of methyl chloroform
>
> are held (see Annex III, Table 2, for a list of the tax rates).
>
> In 1989 the EPA set up a system for trading ODC quotas in order to manage the phase-out of these substances in accordance with the Montreal Protocol. The EPA set a series of declining caps over the period 1989-2000 and allowances for each firm. Trades are possible internationally and within the US – the EPA administers the US programme. A total of 321 million kilograms (561 trades) were traded by firms with the US over the period 1989-1995.
>
> The phase-out of a number of ODCs and the development of ODC substitutes was achieved more quickly than the timetable of the Montreal Protocol. Harrison [in OECD (1999*d*)] suggests that this achievement has more to do with the availability of substitutes and technological change that reduced the costs of phase-out rather than savings due to trading. The role of the ODC tax is hard to determine; the tax was introduced to reduce the windfall profits of those firms allocated allowances.*
>
> ---
>
> *Note:* See Section 8.2.5 for an appraisal of the environmental effectiveness of the CFC tax.
> * The quota system limited the production of CFCs and raised the price of CFCs and the quotas.

enjoys large trade surpluses, a potential difficulty with buying international emission permits on a large scale, to meet domestic emission reduction commitments, is that the outflow of money overseas may be politically sensitive, even if overall emission reduction targets are reached at lower cost.

An obstacle for such a policy mix, is the loss of (potential) tax revenue, if a tradable emission system is established, unless the trading scheme is limited to those sectors currently exempted from any carbon tax, or unless permits are auctioned. For example, the current differentiated CO_2 tax in Norway means that several branches of industry, including the petroleum and private transport sectors, pay relatively high tax rates. The Norwegian Quota Commission (2000) (see Box 8) assumed that the international equilibrium price for a tonne of CO_2 would be US$14 (NOK 125), which is a third of the price paid for CO_2 emissions for petrol sales, under the present tax scheme.[13] Therefore even if the government auctioned permits to those sectors currently paying the CO_2 tax, it might lose revenue, depending on the permit price.

In the UK, trading to meet sector commitments will be possible both between, and within, energy-intensive user sectors, covered by energy efficiency negotiated agreements. In addition, a wider trading scheme, spearheaded by the Emissions Trading Group, has been proposed, and now has government financial support, for further development. This scheme would be open to those companies outside of the negotiated agreements. It is anticipated that trades would be permitted with companies covered by negotiated agreements and eventually with overseas companies.

Box 8.   **Carbon taxes and trading proposals in Norway**

The Norwegian government set up a Quota Commission to investigate a possible domestic carbon-equivalent trading scheme in 1998. In December 1999, the Quota Commission published its recommendations. The most difficult issue to resolve, as with environmentally related taxation, was the impact of emissions trading on the international competitiveness of energy-intensive industry. A quota system that would bring about cost-effective emission reduction would also exert pressures for restructuring on the energy-intensive industries (in Norway: refineries,* metallurgical and chemical producers). A carbon tax levied on these sectors could cause some firms to become unprofitable and close, or relocate overseas. This issue dominated, and split, the Commission, specifically with reference to the allocation of quotas, in particular whether quotas should be auctioned or grandfathered. Grandfathering permits to the energy-intensive industries would overcome the competitiveness issues.

The quota system recommended by the Commission would cover emissions from all sources where it is technically feasible to measure emissions. Emissions that are too costly or impractical to measure can either be regulated by other measures, or remain unregulated. A secondary market is envisaged open to sources not covered by the quota system, and to foreign interests. Subject to Kyoto rules, the participants in the domestic quota system would be able to acquire permits from abroad through the Kyoto flexible mechanisms (see Box 17).

---

*   The inclusion of oil and gas refineries in the scheme, in practice, includes most usage into the system, as refineries
    would pass on the tax to end users.
Source: Quota Commission (1999).

Schreiner [in OECD (1999d)] identifies a potential problem with combing a tax and trade system. If major point source emitters are outside any scheme, for example, electricity generators or the energy-intensive industry sector, then the differential between marginal costs of "abatement" inside and outside the system could be large and inefficiencies in the pattern of abatement would result. Smith [in OECD (1999d)] argues that where taxes and permits are used together, uncertainty over the value of permits is created, affecting incentives to hold permits, including for flexibility mechanisms such as banking.[14]

With the limited experience available it is difficult to assess the practical difficulties of establishing parallel or complementary taxation and emissions trading schemes, and to assess their effectiveness.

2.4.4. *Environmentally related taxation and subsidies*

A difficulty created by the open European electricity market (and by border tax adjustment rules, under the WTO), is that environmentally related taxes, in practice, have to be levied on electricity consumption, rather than on the carbon-content of the primary energy used to generate the electricity. Consequently, the incentive to reduce carbon emissions is weakened, and electricity sourced from renewable energy, is treated the same as coal generated electricity. Hence, such taxation generates no incentives to shift to lower carbon fuel sources. To create such incentives, some countries, *e.g.* Germany and Finland, have introduced subsidies to improve the relative standing of renewable electricity. The UK has also exempted renewable electricity from its tax on industry and business use of energy (2001).

In Japan modelling results indicate that a combination of a carbon tax with the use of its revenues to fund subsidies for investment in large-scale energy conserving technologies, could reduce the economic cost of cutting CO_2 emissions, compared to a pure carbon tax policy [EIEP (2000)]. If the funds from a carbon tax were fully recycled into investment in energy efficient technology, a tax rate of just $27 per tonne of carbon is estimated to be needed to reduce CO_2 emissions by 2% by 2010 from 1990 levels. This compares to a base case pure carbon tax policy levied at $273 and $364 per tonne of carbon.[15]

Environmentally focused subsidies can be complicated to administer to generate incentives for an efficient and cost-effective development of renewably sourced electricity, and energy-efficient investments. To ensure that subsidy funds are distributed efficiently, information on what energy-efficiency investments and/or renewable energies to support, would have to be constantly updated. If not, the programme could offset dynamic incentives. Updating the technology list is likely to be costly. In addition, there is an issue of capital transfer between sectors in the economy, *i.e.* the Japanese simulation found that industry faces a net cost, whilst the transport sector receives a net benefit, from the tax/subsidy package. In addition, for competition reasons, European Union Member states need approval for such subsidies from the European Commission. All subsidies should conform to the PPP (see the Introduction) and therefore must be carefully checked before approval.

2.4.5. *Policy options*

To date there has been limited assessment of the effectiveness of different policy mixes. Evaluation of the impact of individual measures in the policy package is likely to be complicated. However, the UK government in Budget 2000 provided an estimated breakdown of carbon emission reductions by policy measure in the tax on industry and business use of energy package.[16] There are a number of policy packages in climate change policy, *inter alia* because concern over international competitiveness of the most affected sectors and income distribution concerns make it difficult to implement an environmentally effective uniform carbon tax. Additional policies including voluntary agreements, regulations, subsidies, proposals for grandfathered emission permit schemes are then introduced to generate incentives for energy savings/carbon reductions in those sectors benefiting from tax rebates and exemptions. There is a real risk of wasteful policy overlap, increased administrative discretion and inefficient, non cost-effective energy use/carbon emission reduction when economic instruments are saddled with additional policy measures. However, many countries will be interested in situations where policy instruments generate supplementary and complementary incentives and reduce (the perceived) overall emission/pollution reduction costs. In the future, climate change policy could include the following elements: energy/greenhouse gas taxes, regulations, and domestic and international carbon equivalent emission trading.

2.5. Evaluating environmentally related taxation

The OECD/EU database on environmentally related taxes illustrates the variety of activities, products and emissions on which environmentally related taxes and charges are levied. A number of countries have introduced such taxes principally to provide a price incentive to reduce or prevent pollution or to protect natural resources, whilst other taxes are primarily revenue raising instruments. Assessments of the effectiveness of such taxes should include both environmental and economic aspects.

2.5.1. *The evaluation criteria*

A previous OECD study[17] investigated what criteria are relevant for evaluating environmentally related taxation. The study also recommended the introduction of in-built evaluation procedures, including the collection of relevant data, to improve *ex post* appraisal. The criteria identified comprise environmental effectiveness, economic efficiency, dynamic effects, administrative and compliance costs and economy-wide and "soft" effects:

- The *environmental effectiveness* of a tax can be measured as the extent to which the tax delivers its environmental objectives. The quantitative emissions reduction effect of a tax depends on the response of the polluter to the price incentive. These behavioural responses are dealt with more fully in Chapter 8.
- *Economic efficiency* has two aspects. Environmentally related taxes exploit the different opportunities for abatement within a sector, and within an economy, by creating incentives for those firms, or sectors, with the lowest abatement costs to undertake most abatement of the

polluting activity, resulting in an efficient cost-minimising pattern of abatement activity. A measure of economic efficiency is therefore the extent to which the tend to equalise abatement costs across pollution sources.

- It would also be useful to have a measure of *dynamic efficiency*. Environmentally related taxation creates incentives for firms to develop new technologies and techniques that might abate more cheaply, therefore a possible test is to appraise the type and cost of abatement before and after a tax is levied.

- It is important to design environmentally related taxes to achieve environmental and revenue objectives whilst minimising the *administrative costs* of operating the tax. Many environmentally related taxes are added to, or modify, existing taxation in order to reduce administrative costs. However, many taxes, such as on carbon/energy have multiple exemptions and rebates, including rebates linked to negotiated agreements, that may be costly to administer. Administrative costs could be compared to other taxation, for example VAT and to total revenues collected.

- A potential advantage of some environmentally related taxes compared to command and control approaches, is a reduction in *compliance costs* for business or households. Industry can decide how to respond to a tax, whereas with regulation this flexibility is limited. Compliance costs include any extra costs of operating less polluting production technology, and the administrative costs of measuring and verifying compliance. Households may also incur additional expense and loss of utility due to changing consumption patterns.

- The *revenues* raised by a tax on emissions, activity, or product depend on the behavioural response of the taxpayers to the charge. Revenues are not a good indicator of the environmental effectiveness of a tax. If producers respond to a tax by reducing output and/or investing in abatement activities then the taxable item (the emissions) will reduce, as will revenues. If the price elasticity of the taxed product or activity is low (in absolute value), an increased tax rate could cause revenues to increase. The options for, and the potential impact of, revenue recycling on investment, prices, employment and economic activity is discussed in more detail in Sections 1.6 and 2.3.

- Environmentally related taxation will also impact more generally on the economy and on producer and consumer behaviour. It is difficult to disentangle and quantify these *"soft" effects* that may include changes in the general price level, technology mix, employment, international trade, and income distribution and changes in producer or consumer attitudes and awareness of environmental issues. Where possible qualitative information on these effects could be given.

2.5.2. A *case for better evaluations*

Appraisals can either be *ex ante* or *ex post*. An *ex ante* appraisal, undertaken before the implementation of a tax, attempts to predict the environmental and economic impacts of the tax based on previously observed information, specifically price elasticities and abatement cost data. In contrast, *ex post* evaluation attempts to assess all the *observed* responses to the tax after its implementation. Clearly, a combination of *ex ante* and *ex post* evaluation would both enable an assessment of prediction methodologies, the performance of the tax, and its implementation, that could be used to improve the design, implementation and overall effectiveness of the tax instrument. In practice, however, there are very few *ex post* evaluations or systematic assessments of environmentally related taxes. It can be difficult to obtain the relevant assessment data, in part because many taxes are newly implemented. It can also be complicated to disentangle the effect of the taxes operating through the price effect from other complementary policy tools. In addition, it can be difficult to measure the benefits. A good evaluation should include short-term impacts and longer-term effects in order to capture technological and structural change. An in-built process of evaluation would encourage governments to introduce data gathering measures and appropriate mechanisms to evaluate the cost and environmental effectiveness of taxes.

Evaluating the effectiveness of environmentally related taxes leads to a discussion of demand price elasticities (see Section 8.1). In addition, one needs to address the impact on relative prices resulting from the introduction or modification of an environmentally related tax, which will depend on tax incidence. Section 8.2 reviews empirical evidence for the environmental effectiveness of taxes implemented in OECD Member countries.

NOTES

1. Whereby governments utilise measures such as brokered sales contracts, and import restrictions, to ensure domestic producers can charge above market prices for their goods.

2. Subsidies to the coal industry artificially support coal-burn and work against a transition to lower-carbon and more efficient fuels in the electricity generation mix.

3. Subject to clearance from the European Commission, the UK intends to introduce a new subsidy to the coal industry, for a three-year period. At the same time the UK plans to lift its moratorium on the construction of new gas-fired power stations. Ms Helen Liddell, Minister for Energy and Competitiveness in Europe, has stated that the stricter consents policy would be lifted as soon as new electricity trading arrangements are in place.

4. In particular for NO_x and particulates emissions.

5. For example, see ECMT (1998) and ECMT (2000) for estimates of the level of taxation required to internalise the external costs of road transport by fuel.

6. Tax design issues and efficiency criteria are discussed in Sections 1.5 and 2.5.

7. Environmentally related taxation can also generate supplementary environmental benefits, for example a revenue-neutral CO_2 tax, would create incentives to burn less fossil fuels, which in turn would reduce other emissions associated with fossil fuels, for example, SO_2 and NO_x emissions.

8. For a detailed assessment, see Majocchi (1996) and OECD (2000c).

9. General equilibrium models and macroeconomic models.

10. There are also indications that voluntary approaches are likely to generate significant "soft effects" in terms of the dissemination of information, innovation diffusion and awareness raising. However, there is no evidence that these impacts are larger than those that could have been achieved by using a tax instead.

11. The Norwegian Quota Commission (see Box 8) did, however, *not* propose to combine taxes and tradable permits. Instead it proposed a broadest possible quota system, that would replace current CO_2 taxation. Also in Canada a proposal for a quota system has been presented, see TPWG (2000).

12. The international quota price estimated in the Japanese study (US$91 per tonne of carbon) is almost twice as high as that assumed by the Norwegian Quota Commission (US$51 per tonne of carbon).

13. Note that in theory the price of (domestic) permits should equal the present value of the taxes and would produce the same pollution reduction. However, the Norwegian carbon tax is differentiated, not uniform.

14. "Article 3 of the Protocol also provides for *carrying over unused permits into future commitment periods.* The *banking* provision is relevant to the "hot air" issue, since if countries are prevented from selling "hot air" they will automatically be able to carry it over into the future. Banning hot air trading would in this case do nothing to reduce cumulative emissions only delay them somewhat – provided that assigned amounts for future commitments periods are not affected by actual emissions, which in practice they may well be given the sequential nature of negotiations." [Italics added, see OECD (1999b)].

15. If these data are correct, there should be adequate incentives to develop these technologies regardless of a carbon tax.

16. The price effect of the levy is calculated to result in at least a saving of 2 MtC by 2010. The other carbon emission savings are believed to result from other measures: 2.5 MtC from the negotiated agreements and 0.5 MtC from energy efficiency measures.

17. Based on OECD (1997).

Part II

IMPLEMENTING GREEN TAX REFORM

This Part provides a description and assessment of how governments have responded to the various implementation considerations, both when environmentally related taxes have been introduced in isolation, and when they have been introduced as part of wider green tax reforms. Issues that merit further investigation have been singled out, for instance, how to deal with the sectoral competitiveness and distribution of income issues.

Chapter 3

AN OVERVIEW OF GREEN TAX REFORM AND ENVIRONMENTALLY RELATED TAXES IN OECD COUNTRIES

Since the early 1990s, several countries have introduced comprehensive green tax reforms, in most cases in a context of a *constant tax burden*, where new environmentally related taxes have offset reductions in existing taxes. The Nordic countries were forerunners in introducing green tax reforms.

- *Finland* was the first country to introduce taxes specifically targeting CO_2 emissions. A mostly uniform carbon tax on fossil fuels (albeit with exemptions *e.g.* for fuels used as reduction agents in metallurgical processes) was introduced in 1990, but later on additional exemptions and refund mechanisms were introduced to favour energy intensive industries, and taxation of electricity was moved from fuel usage in power plants to the consumption stage. The revenues raised from green taxes have been used to partly offset revenue losses stemming from cuts made in taxes on labour.

- *Norway* followed with a CO_2 tax on mineral oils in 1991. A later "Green Tax Commission" that presented its report in 1996 placed major emphasis on the possibility of achieving a "double dividend". Due to a favourable employment situation when the government presented its follow-up proposal's to the Parliament in 1998, less emphasis was then placed on the double dividend issue; however part of the revenue of these taxes has enabled a reduction in income taxes and increased support for energy saving investments and renewable energy sources.

- *Sweden* introduced a major tax reform in 1991 in a strict revenue neutral context. A significant reduction in income tax was offset by new environmentally related taxes on carbon dioxide and sulphur, by a restructuring of energy taxation and by a broadening of the VAT tax base. At the same time energy taxes levied on industry were significantly reduced. In the budget for 2001, tax increases on diesel, heating oil and electricity was combined with tax cuts, including lower income taxes and social security contributions.

- *Denmark* introduced a CO_2 tax on fuels in 1992 and has been engaging in a general reform of its tax system with a continuing evolution of energy-related taxes planned until 2002. The main objectives of the reform are: the reduction of marginal tax rates in all income brackets; the elimination of a series of loopholes in the tax law; and a gradual transfer of tax revenue from income and labour to pollution and scarce environmental resources [Danish Ministry of Finance (1995)]. However many of these taxes have numerous exemptions and a complicated structure that may reduce their environmental effectiveness.

- The *Netherlands* introduced a general fuel tax in 1988 and a number of other environmentally related taxes, for example on waste, groundwater, and a new regulatory energy tax in 1995 and 1996. A second Green Tax Commission was established in 2000 in order to make proposals for a third round of green tax reform to be implemented in 2001.

- In 1993, *Belgium* introduced a new tax on some energy products which amounted broadly to a tax on the private use of energy. The revenue generated was meant to finance a reduction in employers' social contributions.

After a "first wave" of green tax reforms in the early 1990s in the above countries, other countries have followed:

- In A*ustria*, a waste tax had been implemented in 1989, and an energy tax on gas and electricity was introduced in 1996. The tax rate on electricity was increased in mid 2000. The Länder get a transfer of about 12% and the Communities 5% of the energy tax revenues, to promote measures to protect the environment and to save energy.

- In the UK, a landfill tax came into force in 1996, with revenues allocated to reductions in social security contributions, and a "climate change levy", a tax on industry and business use of energy, will be introduced in April 2001. A tax on virgin sand, gravel and rock is planned for 2002. However, in 2000 the government abandoned its "road fuel duty escalator", which previously had raised the fuel excise duty by 6% annually.

- In 1998, I*taly* adopted a number of environmentally related taxes, including a phased-in CO_2 tax on mineral fuels. The revenues are recycled through reduced rates of social security contributions on labour (60.5%) and compensation measures (31.1%). However, under pressure from increasing world oil prices since 1999, the Italian government has cut excise taxes on oil products, and postponed the tax reform. Italy also has a landfill tax, as well as NO_x and SO_2 taxation.

- *Germany* implemented an ecological tax reform in April 1999. The main goals of the programme are to generate incentives for energy savings[1] and accelerate industrial change, to fund renewable energy programmes, and to increase employment by reducing the burden of labour taxation. The German reforms include phased-in rate rises, for both mineral oils and electricity taxation. For further details on the German tax reform see Box 9.

- In F*rance*, a major restructuring of environmentally related taxes and charges was initiated in 1999. This included a government proposal to extend the *taxe générale sur les activités polluantes* ("general tax on polluting activities") to fossil fuels and electricity. It was in this connection planned to issue tax credits based on a percentage of past emissions. The percentage would have varied according to emission intensity. Substantially modified in Parliament, among other things through the addition of further exceptions and exemptions, the bill was subsequently ruled unconstitutional by the Constitutional Court at the end of 2000.

The S*wiss* electorate rejected two proposals for a green tax reform in a referendum held in September 2000: 1) a tax on all non-renewable energy, the revenues of which would have been used to lower social contributions. 2) a small levy on non-renewable energies earmarked for promoting renewable energy sources and enhancing energy efficiency. However, an incentive tax on fossil fuels will

---

Box 9. **German ecological tax reform**

A recent example of green tax policy is the German tax reform of 1999, which comprised an increase of mineral oil duties and electricity taxes. The extra revenue was used to reduce pensions insurance contributions by 0.8 percentage points (half in employees' and half in employers' contributions). The pensions insurance contributions were reduced from 20.3% to 19.5%, and total social security contributions from 42.3% to 41.5%.

In a second phase of the reform, the tax rate on mineral oil is increased 0.06 DM per litre, and on electricity by 0.005 DM per kWh, annually from 2000 to 2003. The pensions insurance contributions rates were correspondingly reduced by 0.1% in 2000 and will be reduced by a further 0.3% per year for the remaining three years, thus totalling a 1% cut by 2003. Half the reduction will be made in employers' contributions and half in employees' contributions. The tax reform has been an explicit policy of tax shifting, designed to reduce both CO_2 emissions and unemployment.

Source: Official sources and Schlegelmilch (2000).

be implemented on a subsidiary basis, in 2004 at the earliest, if the Kyoto CO_2 reduction targets can not be met by voluntary action and programmes in the industrial sector.

3.1. Revenues from environmentally related taxes[2]

The revenues from (pollution-oriented) environmentally related *taxes* amount to, on average, in the order of 2% of GDP (see Figure 3) and 6% of total tax revenues (see Figure 4). Measured per capita the revenues from these taxes vary between less than $100 to almost $1 700 per year, with an average of about $500 per year (see Figure 5).[3] *The graphs should be interpreted with caution* – and in conjunction with detailed information on the taxes in the various countries. Few – if any – inferences concerning the "environmental friendliness" of the tax system in the countries can be drawn from the graphs below alone. For instance, a low revenue from the taxes in question, could either be due to little use of environmentally related taxes, or due to broad use of such taxes, where high tax rates have caused significant changes in behavioural patterns among producers and consumers (*e.g.* reduced emissions). Also, the share of revenue from environmentally related taxes in total tax revenue is largely influenced by the extent of taxation of non-environmentally related tax-bases. Finally, a country might raise substantial revenues on certain tax-bases by applying lower tax rates than neighbouring countries, and thus attracting customers from these countries.

Although there are differences between countries, the revenues from these taxes are significant in all the Member countries. Denmark is the country where the revenues from the taxes in question constitute the largest share of GDP, while Korea, Greece, Portugal and Turkey are the countries with the largest shares in total tax revenues. The significant contribution of environmentally related taxes in terms of GDP in these countries demonstrates the importance of fuel taxation in their tax systems. Denmark, Luxembourg and Norway are the countries with largest revenues per capita.

Figure 3.   **Revenues from environmentally related taxes in per cent of GDP**

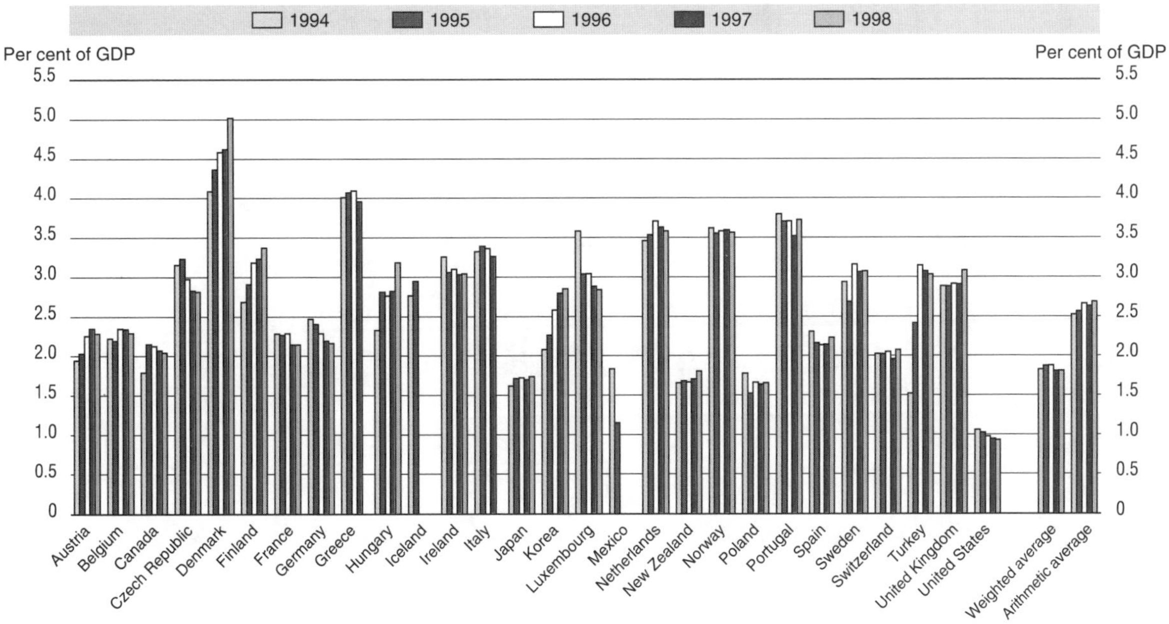

Numbers for France and Luxembourg are low-end Secretariat estimates

Source: The OECD/EU database on environmentally related taxes.

Figure 4. **Revenues from environmentally related taxes in per cent of total tax revenues**

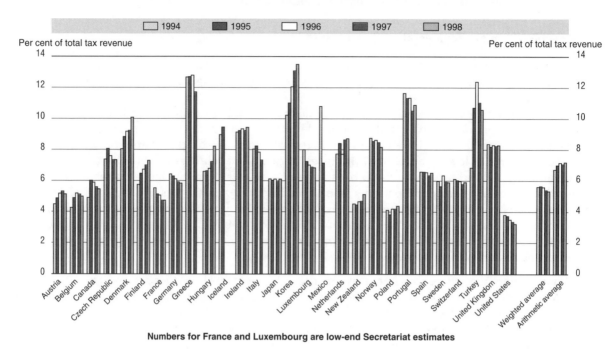

Numbers for France and Luxembourg are low-end Secretariat estimates

Source: The OECD/EU database on environmentally related taxes.

Figure 5. **Revenues from environmentally related taxes per capita**

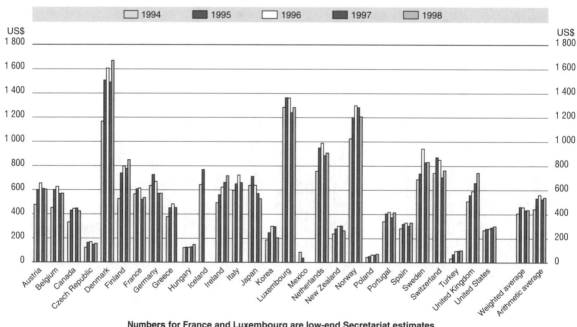

Numbers for France and Luxembourg are low-end Secretariat estimates

Source: The OECD/EU database on environmentally related taxes.

Looking across the period 1994-1998, revenues from environmentally related taxation increased considerably in importance in Austria, Denmark, Finland, Hungary, Korea, the Netherlands and Turkey. A number of factors have contributed to this, among them a broadening of the application of existing taxes to new tax-bases, increases in tax rates and the introduction of a number of new environmentally related taxes. For France, Luxembourg and the United States, the figures indicate a decrease in importance of these revenues.[4]

Figure 6 breaks down environmentally related tax revenue by tax-bases. The figure refers to 1995, the only year for which comparable information is available. The transport sector accounted for 90% of total environmentally related tax revenues, raised from taxes on petrol, diesel fuel and motor vehicles. Note that tax revenues from coal, coke, heavy fuel oil and electricity production were close to zero. The remainder of total environmentally related revenues were raised on such items as natural gas, waste, packaging materials, etc.

The situation seem to have stayed much the same since 1995, with two changes: New or increased waste taxes in a number of countries have increased the revenues raised on waste management considerably, and the disappearance of leaded petrol from the market in many countries has probably lowered the revenues from this tax-base.

Figure 6. **Revenues raised on environmentally related tax-bases**
21 OECD Member countries, 1995

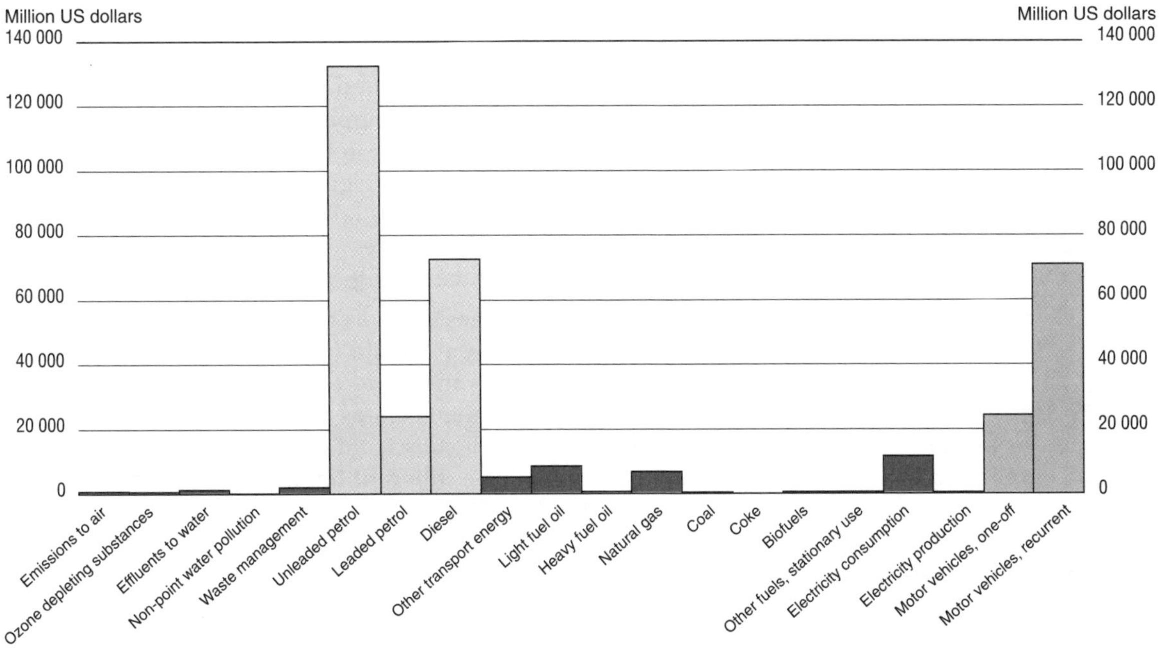

Source: The OECD/EU database on environmentally related taxes.

3.2. Energy and fuel taxes

3.2.1. "Carbon" taxes

Denmark, Finland, Italy, the Netherlands, Norway, and Sweden have introduced levies named "carbon-taxes" or "CO_2-taxes". Although these taxes often cover new, fossil-based tax-bases, and although the tax rates *to some extent* vary according to the carbon content of those fuels that are taxed, the levies are not pure carbon taxes. In particular, numerous exemptions and rebates are applied, reflecting various non-environmental policy objectives, such as concern for sectoral competitiveness or income distribution. To illustrate, energy used in the generation and distribution of electricity is normally exempt from taxation, so is aviation fuel and energy used in commercial fishing. Further, coal and coke used in the production of cement, or used as a raw material – or reduction agent – in industrial processes, is either completely exempt or major refunds can be given.

The following are *examples* of special provisions that apply:

- *Denmark* rebates taxes to registered business depending on the energy intensity of production. For energy used in heavy industrial processes, and where the firm has entered an agreement to undertake energy efficiency improvement investments, 97% of taxes due are refunded. Taxes paid on ultra light diesel and gas used in public transportation are reimbursed, and an additional subsidy of 0.10 DKK (0.014 €) per litre is given.

- In *Finland*, fuels used in industrial production as a raw material or auxiliary material or consumed as immediate inputs in manufacturing of goods are exempt. Further, a firm is eligible for a 85% refund on the amount of tax on energy products that exceeds 3.7% of its value added.

- In the *Netherlands*, refunds can be given when energy sources are not used as fuels. The tax rate on natural gas is lower for those that use more than 10 million m^3 gas per year than for other users.

- In *Norway*, coal and coke used as a reduction agent in industrial processes or used in the production of cement and the building material "Leca" are exempt from taxation. These exemptions represent around 99% of all CO_2 emissions from coal and coke use in Norway. The paper and pulp industry and production of fishmeal pay half the ordinary rates of the CO_2-tax on mineral products.

- In *Sweden*, fuels used for the production of heat in a combined heat and power plant has a reduced energy tax rate of 50%. Fuels that are used for other purposes than as motor fuels or for heating are outside the scope of the tax, and thus exempted. Refunds are given for the whole energy tax and 65% of the carbon dioxide tax when fuels are used in manufacturing industries, agriculture and forestry.. There is also an upper limit on tax payments for these sectors: If the CO_2 tax obligation, after the 65% reduction, exceeds 0,8% of the sales value of the firm, the company only has to pay 24% of the reduced CO_2 tax rate above the ceiling.

In short, even if these levies are often labelled "CO_2 taxes", the tax rates facing different polluters hardly reflect the carbon content of the fuels they are using. It should further be kept in mind that a "fiscal" tax levied on *e.g.* petrol or diesel will have exactly the same economic and environmental impacts as a "CO_2-tax" levied on the same fuels, as long as the tax rates on the different tax-bases are the same. A "proper" carbon tax, where the tax rates on all sources of CO_2-emissions reflected the carbon content of all the fuels used,[5] would, however, have different impacts from a more narrowly based tax.

3.2.2. *Automotive fuels and light fuel oil taxes*

Figure 7 illustrates the tax rates on unleaded petrol, diesel and light fuel oil used for heating purposes in 25 OECD Member countries as of 1.1.2000.[6] All tax rates are expressed in Euro, using average 1999 exchange rates in the calculation.[7] Where there are several tax rates for the product in question – *e.g.* concerning unleaded petrol with different environmental characteristics – the lowest rate is used in the graph.

The graph illustrates total nominal tax rates applicable to unleaded petrol, diesel and light fuel oil respectively, by adding together specific tax rates concerning the "normal usage" of these products. The fact that certain sectors (*e.g.* agriculture) are allowed to purchase fuels at lower tax rates is *not* accounted for, nor are partial refunds given to certain uses,[8] such as in heavy vehicles or in public transport.[9] These exemptions and refunds – which in given cases have large impacts on "effective" tax rates – are, however, described in detail in the OECD/EU database on environmentally related taxes.

Figure 7. **Tax rates on motor vehicle fuels and light fuel oil, as of 1.1.2000**

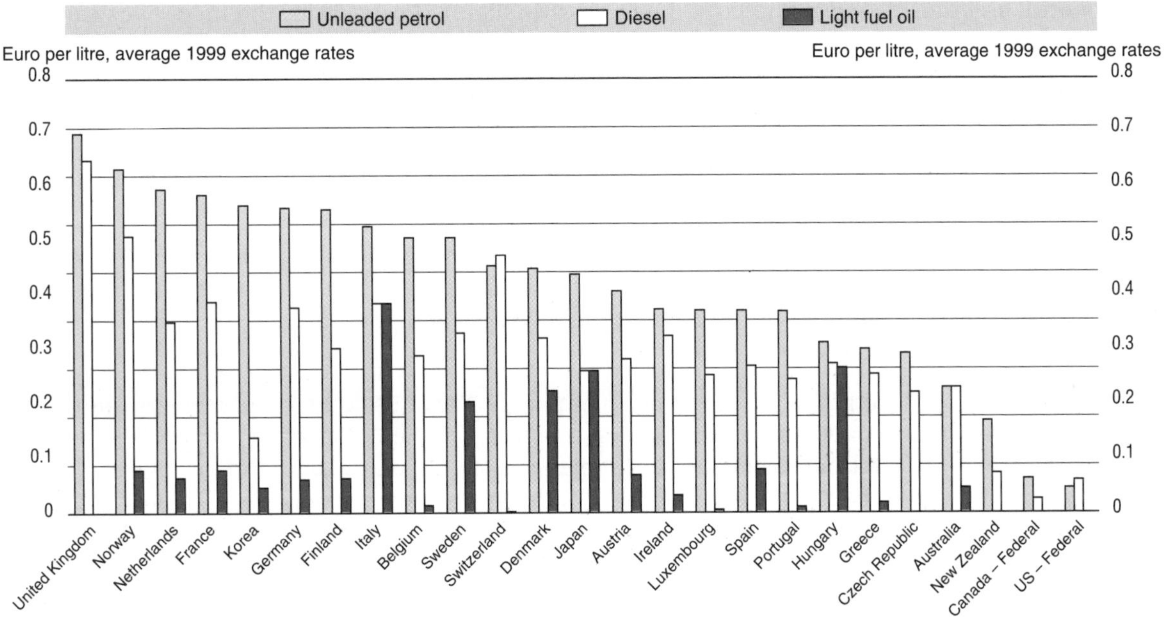

Euro per litre, average 1999 exchange rates

Note: There is no direct taxation of diesel in New Zealand. Instead there is a tax per 1 000 km driven with diesel vehicles, with tax rates depending on the weight of the vehicle. In this figure, an implicit tax rate per litre diesel is given, for a vehicle weighing less than 2 tons, here assumed to consume 125 litre diesel per 1 000 km driven.

Source: The OECD/EU database on environmentally related taxes.

A number of observations can be made concerning Figure 7:

- There are large differences in the tax rates applicable in the Member countries, especially as concerns unleaded petrol and light fuel oil.[10] The difference in the tax levels for petrol and diesel in European and North American Member countries is striking.

- In most countries, the tax rate that applies to unleaded petrol is significantly higher than the rate applying to diesel, with the exception of Australia, Switzerland, UK and the United States. From an environmental point of view, this is unfortunate, as the use of diesel – including the "cleaner" qualities of diesel – is more polluting than the use of petrol, in terms of emissions of particles, NO_x and most VOCs. Diesel-powered vehicles cause lower CO_2-emissions per km driven than petrol-driven vehicles, due to lower fuel consumption, however this is not an argument for a preferential tax treatment, as the drivers benefit directly from this fuel consumption advantage.

- The tax rates on light fuel oil used for heating purposes are normally much lower than the tax rates on diesel, even if the products – technically speaking – are almost identical. In some countries (Canada, New Zealand, the United Kingdom and the United States), there are no taxes on heating oils at all. Low taxes on heating oils are often motivated by equity concerns, as low-income households tend to spend a larger share of their incomes on heating than households with higher incomes. From an environmental point of view, lower tax rates on heating oil than on diesel can be motivated by a number of negative externalities concerning transport activities that are not relevant when the fuel is used for heating (traffic accidents, noise, congestion, etc.). However, taking for example the greenhouse gas and sulphur emissions related to the use of heating oils into account, the *very* large differences in tax rates in some countries raise the question of whether not a reconsideration of the rates could be appropriate.

A few countries can warrant some additional comments:

- The United Kingdom applies the highest tax rates of all countries covered on both unleaded petrol and diesel, and the rate on diesel is only slightly lower. Thus, the incentives provided concerning motor fuels are, from the viewpoint of the environment, better than in most other countries covered in the database. On the other hand, the United Kingdom is one of the few countries with no excise taxes at all of light fuel oil used for heating purposes.[11] This is largely motivated by equity concerns, in part because many low-income households live in poorly insulated houses. Alternative mechanisms, with less detrimental environmental impacts, should be considered to address this problem. (See Chapter 5 below.)

- The situation in Switzerland resembles in some ways that of the United Kingdom. The tax rate applying to diesel is the third highest of all the countries covered, and higher than the rate on unleaded petrol, but the tax rate on light fuel oil for heating purposes is the lowest among the countries that tax light fuel oil at all.

- Hungary applies fairly low taxes on petrol compared to most other countries covered in the database, which in part can be explained by the fact that the comparison in the graph does not correct in any way for purchasing power differences. On the other hand, the tax rate on diesel is almost on par with the tax rates on unleaded petrol, and – most striking – the tax rate on light fuel oil used for heating purposes is only slightly below the rate on diesel. The rate on light fuel oil is among the highest – in absolute terms – among all the countries covered. To the extent that differences in purchasing power between countries explain the fairly low tax rate on unleaded petrol and diesel, the high rate on light fuel oil is remarkable.

- The tax rates on fuel oil used for heating purposes are also very high in Italy and Japan compared to most other OECD Member countries.

It should also be underlined that a number of countries have introduced environmentally related tax rate differentiation among automotive fuels and fuel oils. Historically the most important differentiation has probably been the one between leaded and unleaded petrol. As leaded petrol now has disappeared from the market in most OECD countries – partly due to the tax rate differences, partly due to regulations – the importance of this differentiation has diminished. However, a number of other schemes have been introduced, for example:

- In Denmark, the tax rate on petrol differs depending on whether the petrol station that sells it is equipped with a vapour return system.

- In Norway, there is a special sulphur tax (0.03 € per litre) levied on diesel with a sulphur content above 0.005%. This comes in addition to the ordinary SO_2 tax rate, which however in practice does not apply for the diesel qualities sold in Norway.

- Sweden varies the tax rate between 3 different classes of petrol, and between 3 classes of diesel, according to e.g. the content of sulphur and benzene, density, distillation interval, etc.

- In the United Kingdom, the tax rate on ultra low sulphur diesel is about 0.03 € lower per litre than the tax rate on ordinary diesel. The tax rate on ultra low sulphur petrol is about 0.015 € lower per litre than the rate for ordinary unleaded petrol.

3.2.3. Electricity taxes

A number of OECD Member countries apply taxes on electricity consumption, i.e. per kWh, and not – for example – on the carbon content of the primary fuels used to generate the electricity (see Figure 8). In addition to the countries shown in the figure, Spain levies a tax equal to 4.9% of the price of electricity, on production and import of electricity.

Figure 8. **Tax rates on electricity consumption, as of 1.1.2000**

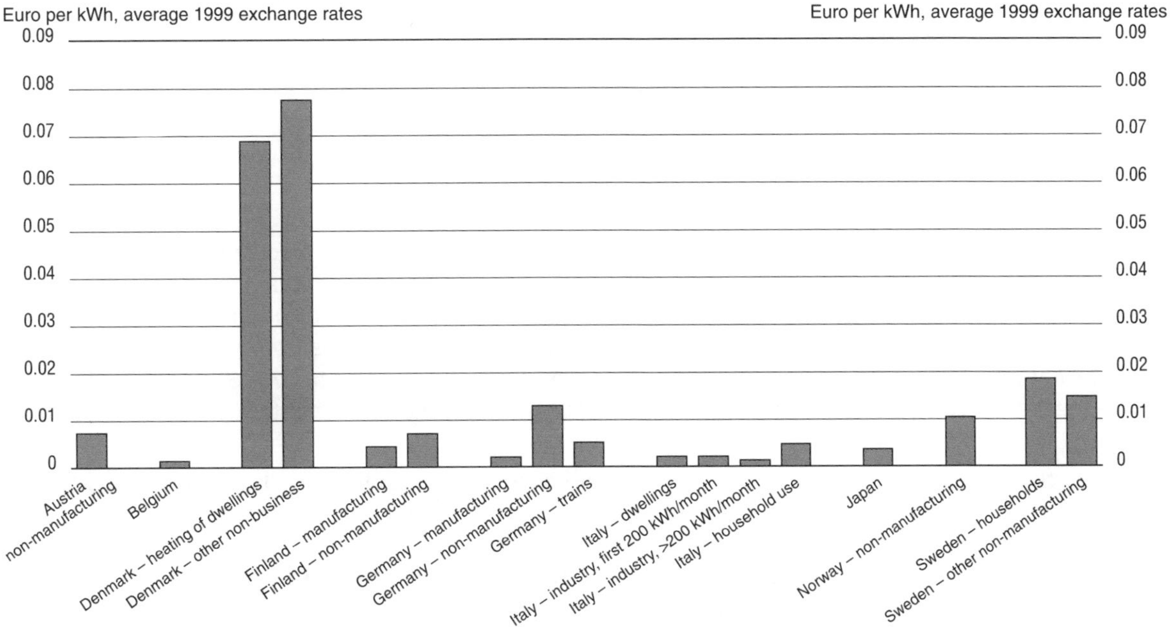

Euro per kWh, average 1999 exchange rates

Bar chart categories: Austria non-manufacturing; Belgium; Denmark – heating of dwellings; Denmark – other non-business; Finland – manufacturing; Finland – non-manufacturing; Germany – manufacturing; Germany – non-manufacturing; Germany – trains; Italy – dwellings; Italy – industry, first 200 kWh/month; Italy – industry, >200 kWh/month; Italy – household use; Japan; Norway – non-manufacturing; Sweden – households; Sweden – other non-manufacturing

Note: Most governments that have implemented electricity taxes have done so with numerous exemptions and rebates. See Box 10 for some examples.
Source: The OECD/EU database on environmentally related taxes.

Due to a large number of exemptions and tax rate differentiations, the rates shown in Figure 8 are not directly comparable. In most cases, taxes on electricity do not apply to the manufacturing (or any industry) sector. If the taxes do cover these sectors, the tax rate is generally lower than for other sectors, important refunds can be given or various types of upper limits on the payments apply. *For example*, in Austria, the energy tax (of which the tax on electricity is one part) is refunded in as so far as it constitutes more than 0.35% of value added of goods-producing firms, if the tax paid amounts to more than 5 000 ATS per year. There are also examples of differences in tax rates between parts of the countries concerned: In Norway (where any use of electricity in manufacturing and in greenhouses is also exempted), electricity use in the northernmost part of the country is not taxed. In northern Sweden, the tax rate is 35% lower than in the rest of the country, except in manufacturing and the greenhouse sector, where the rate is 0 in all the country.

A reason why European countries do not tax input fuels is the competitive pressures of the single European electricity market. In 1996 Finland adjusted its tax on electricity from input use to electricity consumption in order to keep to the single European market rules. These downstream (consumer) electricity taxes are less environmentally effective, *i.e.* they create no incentive for switching to lower or no carbon content fuels, than an optimal upstream tax on input fuels.

3.2.4. *Coal and coke taxes*

Figure 5 illustrated the small contribution coal and coke taxation makes to the total revenue from environmentally related taxes, even though these fuels are heavily polluting and the most carbon intensive. In fact, only Denmark, Finland, the Netherlands, Norway and Sweden levy taxes on coal and coke use at all,[12] and there are *very* important exemptions in the taxes they levy. For instance, as mentioned in Section 3.2.3, coal used for electricity generation is exempted. Further, there are exemptions or refunds when coal and coke are used as a raw material or reduction agent in chemical processes, for any other purpose than heating, or in general when used in businesses/the manufacturing sector. In practice, only a small part of total use of coal and coke in the countries in question is thus affected by the taxes, and hence a simple comparison of the nominal tax rates used has little meaning.

3.2.5. *Aviation fuel taxes*[13]

In 1992 aviation emissions contributed about 3.5% of the total radiative forcing by all anthropogenic activities [IPCC (1999)]. Furthermore, aviation fuel use is projected to increase by 3% per year in the period 1990 to 2015. Aviation also generates other pollutants, for example hydrocarbons and NO_x, causes noise, etc. Nevertheless, aviation fuel is exempt from excise duties in most countries. Rules of the International Civil Aviation Organisation (ICAO) and numerous bilateral Air Services Agreements create legal obstacles to implementing taxes on fuel used in international flights.

Only five OECD countries taxed on aviation fuel or aviation gasoline used on *domestic* flights as of 1.1.2000, see Figure 9. In addition, Canadian provinces and a number of states in the United States levy additional taxes on top of the federal ones shown in the figure. Further, in Norway there is a tax per passenger seat in major domestic and in international flights. Sweden scrapped a previous tax on domestic air traffic in 1997. The tax had two components: one component based on fuel consumption according to engine type and one component based on hydrocarbon and NO_x emissions according to

Figure 9. **Tax rates on aviation fuels used in domestic flights, as of 1.1.2000**

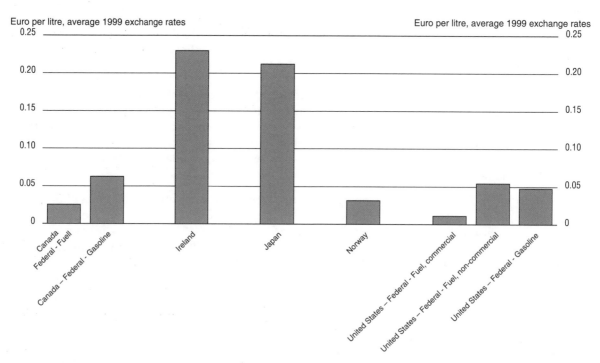

Source: The OECD/EU database on environmentally related taxes.

type of aircraft on an average flight. This tax created incentives for improved engine *design* that reduced HC emissions in the domestically used airplane, the Fokker F28, by 90% [Brännlund (1999)].

In 1999 the European Commission presented the Communication "Air transport and the environment: towards meeting the challenges of sustainable development" (European Commission, 1999), where it was stated that the Commission "will carry out preparatory work with a view to possibly introducing proposals to establish a European Environmental Aviation Charge". Such proposals would be presented in 2001. As a follow-up of the Communication, in 2000 the Commission made a call for tender for feasibility studies of a European Environmental Aviation Charge, based on the distance flown and the environmental performance of the aircraft used, having regard to a wide range of emissions relevant to climate change. The study is to assess *inter alia* the cost-effectiveness of a charge, possible use of revenues raised, as well as legal constraints on the use of such charges.

3.2.6. *Exemptions and refunds in energy and fuel taxes*

As already commented, energy and fuel taxes are not implemented uniformly. Numerous exemptions and rebates apply. They are most often granted to limit impacts on sectoral industrial competitiveness, or to avoid negative impacts on income distribution. Box 10 provide some *examples* of such exemptions andrebates.

Another set of rebates and exemptions in energy and fuel taxes are introduced to promote environmentally friendly products or activities, such as the use of public transportation. For instance, because electricity tend to be taxed at the consumption level (*i.e.* downstream, with all electricity treated the same, regardless of its environmental impacts) some countries have introduced special measures, including tax exemptions, to further the development of, and the proportion of, electricity sourced from renewables.[14] Some *examples* of environmentally motivated exemptions and rebates from and energy taxes are provided in Box 11.

3.3. Other environmentally related taxes

The OECD/EU database on environmentally related taxes also lists a large number of non-energy taxes, the largest sub-sections of which concern motor vehicles, waste and packaging. The next sections provide further details on these taxes.

3.3.1. *Motor vehicle taxes*

Almost all OECD Member countries levy some kind of tax on the sale or use of motor vehicles, and more than half of all the tax bases covered in the OECD/EU database on environmentally related taxes concern such taxes. The tax-bases and tax rates used reflect a number of different policy considerations, including revenue raising, the competitiveness position of the transport sector and any domestic motor vehicle industry, the costs of developing and maintaining the road infrastructure, and – to some extent – environmental impacts of the different vehicles.

One-off vehicle sales or registration taxes are most often differentiated by the weight or engine size of cars and lorries. Such differentiation will generally not be close proxies for the environmental impacts of the vehicles. However, in Austria and the United States (and in the province of Ontario in Canada), vehicle sales taxes are based on more direct environmental criteria, *i.e.* emissions or fuel consumption. For example, the US levies a tax, varying between 1 000 and 7 700 US$ on the sale of energy in-efficient motor vehicles (The "Gas-guzzler tax"), based on the number of miles the vehicle can go per gallon. In Austria, a registration tax – expressed in per cent of the net purchase price – applies to passenger vehicles, and the percentage rate depends on the fuel efficiency of the vehicle. For a petrol-driven and a diesel-driven vehicle using the same amount of fuel per 100 km, the tax rate is higher for the diesel-driven one.[15]

61

Box 10. **Competitiveness based and income distribution based exemptions and rebates in energy taxes**

All countries have numerous exemptions and rebates in their energy and fuel taxes. These provisions are introduced with a number of policy objectives in mind, but will generally reduce the environmental effectiveness of the taxes. A number of *examples* of competitiveness and income distribution based exemptions and rebates are presented below:

For competitive reasons: manufacturing

– **Austria**: the energy tax paid on electricity consumption by the manufacturing industry is refunded if it constitutes more than 0.35% of value added and if the tax paid amounts to more than 5 000 ATS per annum. Mineral oil used in blast furnaces is exempt from the mineral oil tax.

– **Denmark**: businesses registered for VAT can obtain a partial reimbursement of the CO_2 tax paid for electricity, duty on electricity: businesses can gain a rebate on electricity used for other purposes than heating, depending on the energy intensity of the production.

– **Finland**: manufacturing initially paid only 54% of the electricity tax, rising to 61% in 1998. There is an upper ceiling on tax payment and fuels used in industrial production as a raw material or auxiliary material or consumed as intermediate inputs in manufacturing industry are exempt.

– **Germany**: if payments exceed DM 1 000 per year (or over 50MWh electricity) enterprises in manufacturing, agriculture and forestry pay only 20% of the standard rate on electricity and of the tax increase for heating oil and gas. Second if tax payments exceed by 20% the savings made by reduced contributions to the pension insurance, employers can claim a refund.

– **Italy**: there are excise duty rates exemptions for competitiveness reasons, and a lower tax rate for coal use in plants with high-energy capacity.

• **Korea** exempts products used as raw materials for manufacturing of petrochemicals from the transportation and education taxes on petroleum products, and the taxes does not cover products like coal, coke and heavy fuel oil.

• **The Netherlands** applies a tax limit for electricity of 10 million kWh and for natural gas of 1 million m^3.

– **Norway**: Manufacturing industries and the greenhouse sector are exempt from electricity taxes. Coal and coke used as a reduction agent in industrial processes and in the production of cement are also exempt. The pulp and paper industry and production of fishmeal pay half the ordinary rates of the CO_2 tax on mineral products.

– **Sweden**: Refunds are given for the whole energy tax and 65% of the carbon dioxide tax when the fuels are used in manufacturing industries, agriculture and forestry. If the remaining CO_2 tax, after the 65% reduction, exceeds 0,8% of the firm's sales value, the company only has to pay 24% of the reduced CO_2 tax rate above the ceiling. A zero tax rate is also applied on electricity consumed by these sectors.

– **The United Kingdom**: energy-intensive industry that signs up to binding energy efficiency negotiated agreements receives an 80% discount on the climate change levy. Energy used as feedstock or as feed stock and fuel in the same process is exempt, for example, chlor-alkali production and aluminium smelting.

For competitive reasons: energy producers

• Exemptions for energy products produced and consumed at refineries are offered in **Denmark**, **Finland** and **the United Kingdom**.

• Exemptions for energy used for the distribution and generation of electricity are offered in **Denmark**, **Finland**, **Spain**, **Sweden**, and **the United Kingdom**.

For competitive reasons: non-manufacturing

• Exemptions for energy products used in commercial fishing vessels outside territorial waters are offered by **Denmark**, **Finland**, **Norway** and **the United States**.

• Exemptions for electricity and energy used for the production of heat that is delivered for use in commercial greenhouse cultivation are offered by **Sweden** and **the United Kingdom**.

Box 10.   **Competitiveness based and income distribution based exemptions and rebates in energy taxes** (*cont.*)

- **Germany** offers the forestry sector an 80% rebate on the standard rate of the electricity tax and the tax increase in heating oil and natural gas.
- **Italy** offers rebates from fuel excise duties to the commercial transport sector.
- Many countries, including **Belgium**, **Hungary**, **Japan**, **Mexico**, **Switzerland** and **the United States** exempt agriculture from fuel taxes, or provide refunds with similar effects.
- **The Netherlands** offers rebates to horticulture. **Finland** gives partial rebates to commercial greenhouse cultivation.

For income redistribution reasons: households

- **Germany** offers a 50% rebate on the electricity tax for off-peak storage heaters, installed before April 1999. Such heaters are concentrated in low-income households.
- **The Netherlands** has a zero rate band for households consumption of 800m^3 natural gas per year and 800kWh electricity per year.
- **The United Kingdom** exempts domestic use of energy.

For income redistribution reasons: regional

- **Norway** exempts the regions of Finnmark and northern Troms from the electricity tax. In **Sweden**, the tax rate on electricity is about 35% lower in the northern parts of the country than elsewhere.
- **Italy** provides compensation measures for disadvantaged regions.

Source: OECD/EU database on environmentally related taxes and official sources for Italy and the UK.

The tax-bases used in annual taxes on vehicle usage (weight, engine size, the number of axles, etc.) are also seldom close proxies to the environmental impacts caused by the vehicles. However, in Austria, Denmark, Germany and Norway, there are annual usage taxes based on more direct environmental impacts. For example, Denmark levies an annual passenger car fuel consumption tax according to the fuel efficiency of vehicle. The tax rates vary between 440 and 16 100 DKK (about 60-2 170 €) per year for petrol-driven vehicles and between 1 720 and 22 020 DKK (about 230-2 960 €) per year for diesel-driven passenger cars. In Austria, Germany and Norway, the tax rates depend on the environmental class the vehicle belong to, as defined by European Union classifications.

3.3.2. *Taxes on the final treatment of waste*

A number of countries have introduced taxes related to the final treatment of waste and/or on packaging and certain specific products that can cause special waste-related problems. For instance, some European countries have responded to European Union targets on packaging and waste to landfill by implementing such taxes. The taxes discussed in this section come in addition to user charges concerning waste collection, which are levied in most OECD Member countries.[16] Secondary benefits of waste-related taxes can be large, specifically in terms of reduced methane gas emissions (see Chapter 9 for more detail).

Box 11. Environmentally motivated exemptions and rebates in energy and fuel taxes

Governments may also introduce exemptions and rebates in energy taxation for environmental reasons. A number of *examples* are presented below.

For supporting renewable energy sources

- **Denmark** exempts electricity produced by wind or water power from its electricity tax.
- **Finland** refunds electricity production by wind, wood and waste gas from metallurgical processes.
- **Germany** offers exemptions for electricity produced by hydro, deposit gas/biomass, geothermal and wind power from electricity taxation.
- **The Netherlands** exempts electricity generated from renewable energy from its regulatory energy tax, based on the newly introduced certification system for green electricity.
- **Sweden** exempts electricity produced in a wind power plant from energy taxes.
- **The United Kingdom** offer exemptions for "new' renewable energy sources (excludes large-scale hydro) from the climate change levy.

For supporting CHP, district heating and energy efficiency measures

- In **Austria**, a refund of 2.94 ATS (0.21 €) per litre is given for diesel used in combined heat and power stations and in heat pumps
- **Denmark** returns a portion of CO_2 tax revenues to industry in the form of investment support for energy saving.
- **Finland** offers an exemption on the excise on fuels for electricity consumed exclusively by the producer.
- **Germany** exempts combined heat and power plants with an annual utilisation level of 70%. Other heat-power-combination systems with an efficiency of at least 60% are exempt from mineral oil tax increases. Electricity generated for own consumption from small facilities, with a capacity of up to 2MW (in particular district heating plants) is exempt from the electricity tax.
- **Sweden** offers exemptions for electricity produced in a combined heat and power plant and used by producer.
- **The United Kingdom** gives exemptions for efficient combined heat and power generation from the climate change levy. Further, funds are made available from the £50 million "energy efficiency fund' to promote the development of energy efficient technologies and new renewable energy sources. An additional £100m will are made available for enhanced tax allowances for businesses investing in energy saving technologies

For supporting rail and public transportation

- **Austria** exempts LPG for local transport buses and provides a refund of 2.94 ATS (0.21 €) per litre for diesel used in railway engines.
- **Denmark** reimburses CO_2 taxes paid by public transportation, and an additional subsidy of 0.10 DKK (0.013 €) per litre is given.
- **Finland** exempts rail transportation from the electricity tax.
- **Germany** offers local public transport a 50% refund on the electricity tax and the mineral oil tax increase. LPG vehicles benefited from a 60% reduction in 2000.
- **Sweden** applies exemptions for electricity used in trains and other means of transportation on railroads.
- **The United Kingdom** exempts electricity used by public transportation from the climate change levy.
- **The United States** exempts school buses and qualified local buses from federal and state fuel taxes.

Source: The OECD/EU database on environmentally related taxes and official sources for Italy and the United Kingdom.

Figure 10. **Tax rates on final waste treatment, as of 1.1.2000**

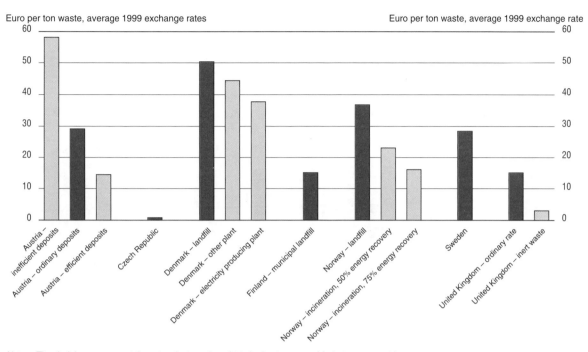

Note: The dark bars represent the rates that are thought to be best comparable between countries.
Source: The OECD/EU database on environmentally related taxes.

Figure 10 shows that a number of governments have introduced differentials in taxes on the end treatment of waste. For example, Austria has different tax rates for landfill depending on the efficiency of the facility, *i.e.* whether it has methane recovery or not. Denmark has set different rates of taxation between incineration and landfilling; landfilled waste is charged at a higher rate than incinerated waste, and between incineration facilities; with lower rates applied to waste deposited at facilities with energy recovery. These tax differentials change the relative prices of final waste treatment options creating differential incentives for different waste streams and between facilities based on the efficiency of the facility, thereby better reflecting the environmental damage of different waste management options.

As with energy taxation, rebates and exemptions are applied to waste taxation. In Box 12 some *examples* of such rebates and exemptions have been separated into two broad categories: Those that relate to sectoral competitiveness and those that are environmentally motivated. Among those in the latter category, the United Kingdom introduced an exemption for inert waste used in the restoration of landfill sites in 1999, because the landfill tax had been so effective in reducing this waste stream to landfills that the restoration of andfill sites was adversely affected.

3.3.3. *Packaging taxes*

A number of countries have also introduced taxes to reduce packaging use and packaging waste. For example, Belgium, Denmark, Finland and Norway (and the provinces of Manitoba and Ontario in Canada) have taxes on beverage containers. Further, Denmark, Korea and Norway tax other packaging

65

Figure 11. **Taxes on beverage containers**

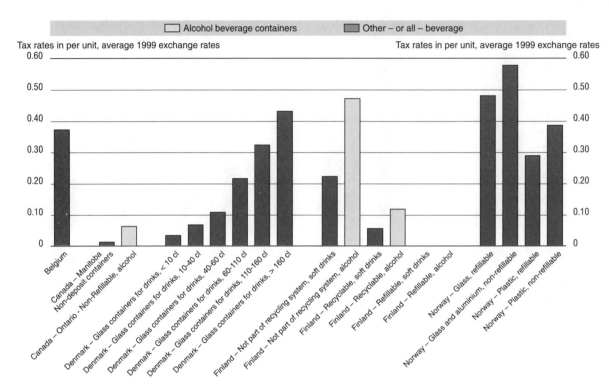

Note: Denmark only sells beverages in glass containers. The Finish tax – imposed (with the same rate) on alcohol beverages and soft drinks only – is based on per litre of beverage. To estimate a per unit tax, it was assumed that alcohol containers contain 0.7 litre and that containers for soft drinks contain 0.33 litre. Denmark and Norway exempt containers for liquid milk from their product taxes on beverage containers. Norway also exempts containers for lemonades. Denmark applies rebates for certain glass containers if their content meets certain requirements and the containers in question are recycled in glass production. Norway has one tax (0.1) per unit that apply to all non-refillable beverage containers, and one tax that depend on the type of material used and on the degree of recycling. Beverage containers that are part of a return system with rates above 95% are completely exempt from this tax, while reduced rates apply for containers being part of any deposit-refund system with a return rate above 25%.
Source: The OECD/EU database on environmentally related taxes.

containers, with different tax rates for different materials used in the container. Differential tax rates can also create incentives for reuse and recycling of packaging material, for example in Norway only non-refillable beverage containers are taxed, and in Finland rates depend on whether or not the container is recyclable or part of a return system. Figure 11 illustrates taxes on beverage containers in operation in OECD Member countries.

3.3.4. *Sulphur taxes*

Tax measures have been also been implemented to reduce SO_2 emissions. Several countries have different rates in taxes on mineral products for fuels with high or low sulphur content. Examples concerning motor vehicle fuels are given in paragraph 138 above. Other countries have such rate differentiation concerning taxes on heavy fuel oil.

In addition, the Czech Republic, Denmark, Norway and Sweden levy separate taxes to the sulphur content of fuels used and/or on measured SO_2 emissions (see Figure 12), whereas Korea levies an air

Figure 12. **Tax rates on sulphur content in fuels, as of 1.1.2000**

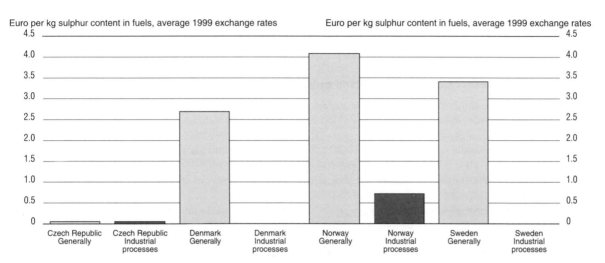

Note: This figure does not include sulphur taxes levied on liquid transport fuels. The Danish sulphur taxes are either levied on the sulphur content of fuels, or on measured emissions of sulphur dioxide (with a tax rate of 1.35 per kg SO_2 emitted). Rebates are given in Denmark to businesses that pay excise duty on the sulphur content of the energy products it used if the sulphur is bound in the ashes. For businesses there is no duty on mineral oils used for technical purposes. In Norway and Sweden there are rebates for proven emission reductions as the result of scrubbing, etc. Norway offers an exemption for oils (not diesel) with a sulphur content of less than 0.05%, in Sweden the limit is 0.1%. In Norway, the verage general tax rate is about 4.1 per kg sulphur, while a lower rate of 0.7 apply on coal and coke, and on mineral oils used in i.a. the pulp and paper industry. Sweden offers complete exemptions for fuels not used in motors or for heating, *i.e.* for industrial use.
Source: OECD/EU database on environmentally related taxes.

pollution charge that covers sulphur emissions. The tax rates per kg sulphur is of comparable magnitude in Denmark, Norway and Sweden, while significantly lower in the Czech Republic. In Denmark, Norway and Sweden, special provisions are in place for fuels used in industrial processes, whereas this seems not to be the case in the Czech republic.

3.3.5. Other taxes

A number of other environmentally related taxes and fees/charges are in place in OECD Member countries *e.g.* concerning the use of certain chemicals and the extraction of use of some natural resources. Box 13 provides some *examples* of such taxes. More details can be found in the OECD/EU database, available at *http://www.oecd.org/ env/policies/taxes/index.htm.*

Box 12. Rebates and exemptions in taxes concerning final treatment of waste

Like for energy taxes, a number of exemptions and rebates apply to waste taxes implemented in OECD Member countries. Some *examples* are presented below:

Cost/competitiveness motivated rebates and exemptions

- **Finland** exempts soil and stone, fly ash and desulphurisation waste from power plants, and waste resulting from industrial production which is deposited on private landfill sites run by the plants.
- **Sweden** exempts earth, gravel, clay, slate, limestone, and other kinds of stone being deposited on special landfills not used for other waste. Waste sand from mining processes being deposited on special landfills not used for other waste is also exempted from taxation.
- **Norway** reimburses the additional charge applicable for delivery of waste to incineration plants, depending on the degree of energy recovery at the plant.
- **The United Kingdom** exempts waste from the dredging of harbours and inland waterways, waste from the reclamation of contaminated land from the landfill tax.

Environmental policy motivated rebates and exemptions

- **Finland** exempts biological waste and sewage sludge, which are delivered to a landfill for composting.
- **Sweden** exempts some types of waste for which there at present are no environmentally acceptable alternatives to land filling, *e.g.* asbestos, contaminated soils, sludge from certain chemical processes etc.
- **The United Kingdom** offers an exemption for inert waste used in the restoration of landfill sites. There are further tax credits in the landfill tax to registered site operators who make contributions to approved environmental bodies. Credits may be claimed to the value of 90% of contributions, to a limit of 20% of the trade's annual landfill tax liability.

Source: The OECD/EU database on environmentally related taxes.

Box 13. Taxes on chemicals and on resource extraction

Environmentally related taxes are also levied on certain chemicals and on some types of resource extraction or use. Some *examples* are presented below.

Chemicals and oil shipping

- **Denmark** and **Norway** both levy taxes on chlorinated solvents. In Denmark, tetrachloroethylene, trichloroethylene and dichloromethane are all taxed 0.27 € per kg net weight of the substance, whilst in Norway the first two chlorinated solvents are taxed 6.0 € per kg of substance.
- **Switzerland** taxes volatile organic compounds (VOCs).
- **Finland** imposes an oil damage levy, with a rate of 0.74 € per ton for oil transported in vessels without a double bottom, and 0.37 € per ton for oil transported in vessels with double bottom.
- **The Czech Republic, Denmark, Finland, Hungary, Italy, Norway** and some states in **the United States** levy taxes or charges on lubricant oils.

Pesticides and fertilisers

- **Belgium , Canada, Denmark, Finland**, and **Norway** levy taxes on pesticides.
- **The Netherlands** has a minerals accounting system, whereby surplus phosphate, above 10 kg per hectare, is taxed 4.54 € per kg and surplus nitrogen is taxed 0.68 € per kg per hectare.
- **Sweden** levies a tax on fertilisers, with rates 0.2 € per kg nitrogen and 3.4 € per gram cadmium.
- **The United States** levies a charge on fertilisers with rates varying from 0.9 to 3.7 € per ton of product.

Water

- **The Netherlands** has a groundwater tax with rates being 0.16 € per m^3 for drinking water companies 0.12 € per m^3 for other companies and 0.05 € per m^3 for a combination of river bank filtration and artificial recharge. Taking into account rebates, a net tariff of 0.03 € per m^3 is charged for the extraction of artificially recharged water. There is also a tax on water supply, at the rate of 0.13 € per m^3.

Mineral extraction

- **Finland** levies a control fee on gravel abstraction.
- **Sweden** levies a tax on natural gravel and the rate is SEK 5 (0.55 €) per ton.
- **The United Kingdom** prepares a tax on the extraction of mineral aggregates from quarries (2002).
- In several states in **the United States**, there are severance taxes on coal extraction (as well as on oil and gas extraction, which generally are not included in the database on environmentally related taxes).

Source: OECD/EU database on environmentally related taxes.

NOTES

1. The taxes are expected to make a significant contribution to the German commitment, to reduce CO_2 emissions by 21%, by the year 2005, compared to 1990 levels.

2. This and the following sections draw to a large extent on the OECD/EU database on environmentally related taxes, which can be found at *http://www.oecd.org/env/policies/taxes/index.htm.*

3. In Figures 3-5, revenues from fees and charges are not included, in part because of lack of revenue data on many of these levies. Neither do they include value added taxes paid on environmentally related tax-bases or taxes. To the extent that VAT is applied consistently across goods and services, VAT has few environmental impacts. However, differences in the treatment of goods and services within a VAT system may have environmental impacts.

4. It is, however, emphasised that for Luxembourg and (in particular) for France, the figures represent low-end Secretariat estimates.

5. Corrections would also have been made for any binding of carbon in products produced, etc.

6. Leaded petrol is not included in the graph. This is because leaded petrol has virtually disappeared from the market in many of the countries concerned – in part because of the tax differences applied, but also due to regulations, *e.g.* concerning the use of catalytic converters in new vehicles, which only can function with unleaded petrol. LPG is, for practical reasons, also not included, although in several countries it is widely used. Finally, light fuel oil used for industrial purposes is not included. This is because here the effective tax rates in many countries differs widely between sectors and specific uses, making a simple comparison almost impossible.

7. No attempt is made to take differences in purchasing power in the respective countries into account.

8. One refund mechanism *is* reflected in the graph: In the Czech Republic, the nominal tax rate on light fuel oil used for heating is equal to the tax rate on diesel. The whole tax payment is however refunded, thus a zero tax rate is used in the graph.

9. For example, in the Netherlands, a refund of 0.02 € per litre is given on diesel oil for lorries with a maximum safe load of over 12 000 kg. In Denmark, taxes paid on ultra light diesel used in public transportation are reimbursed, and an additional subsidy of 0.014 € per litre is given. In Ireland, diesel used in licensed passenger road services is effectively taxed at 0.023 € per litre, instead of the "normal" rate of 0.326 € per litre.

10. The somewhat lower variation in the tax rates for diesel is probably related to the fact that diesel-powered lorries can travel several thousand km when their tanks are filled up. For lorries involved in international transport there is thus a significant potential for "tank tourism" – *i.e.* for buying fuel in countries with lower tax rates.

11. In addition, a preferential VAT-rate of 5% apply to "domestic energy use". (Rate differentiation in value added taxes is generally *not* covered by the database.) Further, the new "Climate change levy" only apply to businesses use of energy.

12. In addition, some states (for example, Alabama and Arkansas) and counties in the United States levy severance taxes on coal extraction.

13. EEA (2000) includes a fuller discussion of issues pertaining to the taxation of aviation.

14. Subsidy schemes implemented in European Union countries have to comply with European Commission guidelines on state aid.

15. The formula used to calculate the tax rate in per cent of the net purchase price is ((Litre petrol/100 km) – 3) x 2 for petrol-driven vehicles and ((Litre diesel/100 km) – 2) x 2 for diesel-driven ones. Thus, for example, for a petrol-driven car that uses 8 litre petrol per 100 km, the tax rate is (8 – 3) x 2 = 10 per cent of the net purchase price. For a diesel-driven car that uses 8 litre diesel per 100 km, the tax rate would be (8 – 2) x 2 = 12 per cent of the net purchase price. For both categories of vehicle, the maximum tax rate is 16%.

16. The design of such user charges can have major impact on the amounts of waste generated. In Switzerland households are obliged to pack their waste in 5 kg plastic bags which are sold for 1.5 CHF (0.9 €) each. In Korea, the waste collection fee is included in the price of plastic bags that are sold – at varying prices – by local governments. According to recent study (EPA, 2001), more than 4 100 communities in the United States have implemented variable rate programmes, where the charges depend on the volume or weight of the waste collected. In most cases where such programmes have been introduced, the amounts of waste collected have decreased significantly.

Chapter 4

ADDRESSING COMPETITIVENESS CONCERNS OVER ENVIRONMENTALLY RELATED TAXATION

4.1. Introduction

A key issue – one often at the core of opposition to the introduction of environmentally related taxes and behind pressures for tax relief – is the threat of reduced international competitiveness in the most affected sectors. Where the introduction of environmental taxes forces higher prices on internationally traded goods, tending to make exports less attractive and imports more so, domestic production generally would be expected to decline, at least in the short run, implying job losses and other economic shocks to the economy. This issue raises important questions over the identification of instances where such dislocations can be expected, their magnitude, possible technological and factor market adjustments over time, and appropriate policy responses. At the same time it forces a reconciliation of environmental objectives and possible implications, including reduced investment and employment in certain sectors, with other economic and public policy goals. Important questions also arise as to whether unilateral efforts towards environmental protection could be strengthened through greater co-operation amongst countries contending with similar competitiveness pressures.

To take an example, a carbon tax is a way of increasing fossil fuel costs to encourage energy conservation through reduced demand for fossil-fuel intensive goods and services (under higher tax-inclusive prices reflecting environmental costs), and substitution towards more environmentally friendly technologies and processes. Adjustment towards the development of, and move to, cleaner technologies and processes may, however, impose significant additional business costs that cannot be passed on through higher output prices or lower returns to labour or capital. While tax incidence effects would vary depending on the particular output market and country situation, in some cases substitution possibilities to avoid environmental taxes simply may not be feasible in the short- to medium-term. It is therefore necessary to analyse what the desired outcome is from a public policy perspective, and the conditions under which these outcomes can be expected to materialise (*e.g.*, where a carbon tax successfully induces firms to innovate, or instead relocate) and to study how competitiveness in the international market is affected by the introduction of a carbon tax, with and without domestic market protection measures (*e.g.*, border tax adjustments), and with or without similar tax measures being adopted by other countries.

Sorting out when environment taxes might involve economic losses and identifying instances where possible adverse effects may be overstated is a complex and difficult issue. Important yet usually contentious questions include the incidence of environmental taxes (including price effects), the existence or not of above-normal profit rates, production and process substitution possibilities, and short- and long-run demand and supply elasticities. Possible positive impacts on non-targeted businesses should also factor in. Each of these areas has been the subject of much attention and research, yet finding answers to these basic questions, let alone understanding how the various factors together impact on the economy, is challenging to say the least.

Indeed, uncertainty over economic effects may encourage governments to provide exemptions and other concessions to business in cases where in fact competitiveness problems for a given sector or activity are not overriding, or more generally where the economy as a whole would benefit from a more environmentally supportive position on the part of government. However, in other cases, competitiveness concerns may be well founded and call for one or more measures to ease implementation.

In this chapter we consider what basic economic theory suggests as the likely economic effects of introducing environmental taxes, taking a tax on fossil fuels (a carbon tax) as an example. We also consider a sampling of evidence regarding the impacts of environmental taxation in practice. It turns out that possible negative effects on business competitiveness have been largely avoided to date on account of generous relieving mechanisms, including tax exemption and rebate provisions reviewed in Section 4.3.

As discussed earlier in the report, the database shows that all OECD countries that have introduced CO_2 and energy taxation have applied differentiated tax rates and offered some sectors and products complete exemptions in order to mitigate any negative impacts on the competitive position of domestic industry and some other economic sectors.[1] This raises not only the question of whether governments have been too quick to offer these to industries that pollute the environment the most, but also whether the most efficient mitigation practices are being followed. It is important to ask, as we consider briefly in Section 4.4, whether better mitigation measures might be found, in particular ones that encourage restructuring towards improvements to the environment.

Finally, in Section 4.5 we pose the question of whether environmental objectives could be furthered if OECD countries were to work more closely in their efforts, with the benefit of such co-operation helping to allay competitiveness concerns. In this discussion, a key consideration is what form this increased co-operation might take and what the focus might be (*e.g.*, information sharing and best practice assessment generally, or on environmental policies concerning polluting activities that have global (and not just local) effects and consequences).

4.2. Possible economic implications – the case of a carbon tax

In examining the business competitiveness issue, certain general predictions can be made. Competitiveness concerns are likely to be greatest where an environmentally related tax is imposed on products or key factors of production where the goods are traded widely in the international market without import protection or other border tax adjustments. Substitution possibilities are also a critical factor, as limited scope for identifying and financing cleaner production technologies and processes implies an inability to substitute away from environmental taxes. Where the introduction of the tax forces higher prices on products directly or indirectly by increasing operating (factor) costs, this tends to weaken the current account position of the country. Demand for exports would be expected to fall, while import demand would be expected to rise, with import prices relatively more attractive following the unilateral adoption of the tax. In short, the imposition of an environmental tax at a significant rate on products tied to the international goods market, with limited substitution possibilities, would be expected to lead to a reduced ability of domestic firms to compete for domestic and foreign market share.

In contrast, competitiveness concerns are likely to be less pressing where an environmental tax is levied on a product or service that cannot be readily imported or exported (*e.g.*, a tax on landfill) and where substitution possibilities are feasible. Where domestic markets are protected by tariff or non-tariff barriers (*e.g.*, import taxes) that make foreign purchases less of a threat and domestic demand for the product relatively inelastic, and where border tax adjustments also apply to export markets, imposing an environmental tax on domestic suppliers may not directly undermine that sector's competitiveness. Partly for this reason many countries tax fuel consumption at the pump. However, where a product or service is exported, or is used in the domestic production of other exported goods or services, the imposition of an environmental tax may have negative implications on export markets, at least in the short run.

Another key consideration is the use of environmental tax revenues. If the revenues are recycled back to the business sector(s) subject of the tax, then job losses and plant closures and thus pressures on government against such taxes may not be as great. This of course depends on how the funds are recycled back to business, under what conditions and for how long. Also, depending on the specific manner in which the revenues are recycled, abatement incentives may be reduced or undone under this approach. Similarly, where the tax revenues are used to lower payroll taxes or employee social security contributions, business costs may not rise to the same extent, at least insofar as the burden of these taxes tends to fall primarily on employers (through higher labour costs). In contrast, such offsets to competitiveness concerns generally would not be expected where environmental tax revenues are used to finance additional government spending on general public services, finance a general income tax rate cut, or lower the government deficit.

Clearly, a thorough examination of the various possible considerations and their interaction over time is beyond the scope of this paper, particularly in light of the fact that responses would tend to differ across OECD countries with diverse industrial and existing policy structures. However, it is useful to place the general discussion in context by considering what basic economic theory has to say as regards the "first round" economic implications.

Take, as an example, the imposition of a carbon tax (while recognising that other product or emissions taxes could also be usefully addressed), and consider first the implications to fuel-consuming firms, for example in the steel industry, operating under imperfectly competitive conditions. In other words, consider first the case where some scope exists for domestic firms to set higher output prices in response to higher input prices (see Annex I for an elaboration). Where a small number of firms dominate the sector, setting output so as to maximise economic profits, the introduction of a carbon tax would generally result in an increase in output prices and a reduction in output of those firms.[2] This result could be expected where the domestic market is protected from foreign competition, or where domestic firms are price-setters on international markets by virtue of special firm characteristics or assets. The main impact of a carbon tax in these cases would be price increases accompanied by output reductions (as opposed to plant closures), reduced fuel consumption, and improvements to the environment.

The increase in the output price means that some part of the burden of the tax is shifted onto consumers of the firm's output, with a larger tax burden shift (*i.e.*, a larger price increase) the more inelastic is the demand for the output produced. Part of the burden of the tax would also fall onto labour, where job losses and/or wage reductions result from the scaling back of output.

In the long run, the post-tax cost structure would depend on the firm's ability and profit incentive to substitute away from the taxed factor in favour of untaxed factors that could be used in the production process. Given the existence of pure economic rents following (and before) the introduction of the tax, the incentive to invest in R&D to avoid the carbon tax might be less than what one would observe under more competitive market conditions.[3]

However, profit maximising incentives would be expected to encourage the affected firms to undertake R&D in pollution abatement. In theory, pollution abatement would be expected up to the point where the marginal benefit of an additional unit of R&D equals its marginal cost. Thus, even in the case where the existence of pure economic rent mitigates the potential for plant closures or relocation, a cleaner environment would be anticipated on account of both output reduction and technological change.

Under more competitive market conditions, where output (*e.g.*, steel) prices are largely fixed in world markets, a carbon (factor) tax would initially result in post-tax operating losses and a reduction in firm-level output. This assumes that the tax does not apply to steel imports, for example due to the administrative difficulties associated with, and the international rules (*e.g.*, WTO) restricting the application of, border tax adjustments in respect of foreign production processes, including fossil fuels consumed in production. With reduced output in the short-run, the difference between domestic supply and demand would be made up by steel imports. Thus, there would be some exporting of production and thus a shifting of the source of the pollution to other countries in the short run.

Over time, and in the absence of technological change, the realisation of economic losses would lead to plant closures as investors withdraw investment capital from the sector generating after-tax rates of return falling below rates expected by shareholders. At the same time, pollution levels linked to domestic production would continue to fall. The loss in domestic production and employment would be accompanied by reduced domestic exposure to pollution damage, to the extent that the latter is local in nature. Where instead the pollution is global in nature (*e.g.*, greenhouse gases), relocation of the production activity would not be similarly balanced by these benefits. The domestic economic effects in the short and long run would depend on environmental policies adopted abroad.

Importantly, plant closures could be limited where firms are able to adopt technologies allowing for a substitution away from fossil fuels to avoid the factor tax. Indeed, a key advantage of a carbon (factor) tax is the dynamic efficiency that it offers, creating incentives for firms to change production processes away from relying on fossil fuels.[4] Technological change that avoids the carbon tax would lower tax-inclusive production costs over a range of output levels, tending to eliminate economic losses on account of the tax. A key, but clearly difficult, issue to resolve is whether costs of technological change can be absorbed without precipitating plant closures. From a policy perspective, this raises the question of how much support is available to business, through R&D tax incentives and other government support, to facilitate technological change, and whether such support is counter-productive or instead supportive of environmental goals.

Where the competitiveness of a firm refers in a strict sense to its ability to produce a given level of output of a given specification and quality at a competitively low output price, it can be said that the carbon tax in certain cases reduces the competitiveness of domestic firms. While this claim is undoubtedly true in certain cases, two points are worth remembering when assessing the impact of an environmentally related tax on a particular sector. First, pure "textbook" conditions rarely apply and environmental taxes are one of a number of factors determining a firm's overall competitiveness.[5] Second, output reductions of polluting activities are often a central goal of environmental reform, and opportunities often exist for consumers to shift their consumption towards near substitutes of goods or services that can no longer be profitably supplied post-tax reform.

On the first point, energy-intensive firms that produce from a given location may have certain location-specific cost advantages relative to other possible sites, suggesting a positive amount of economic rent prior to the introduction of the tax. These advantages could provide some cushion that would permit the introduction of a carbon tax that would reduce profit, but without generating overall economic losses in the sector.[6]

Considering the second point, where the competitiveness of certain firms is negatively affected and output is reduced and accompanying jobs are lost, it is important to recall that reduced domestic production/use of environmentally-damaging products is an intended outcome of a policy decision to use taxes to ensure that the social costs of polluting are reflected in market prices and behaviour. In particular, the intention behind environmental policies is to reduce demand for the production of goods and services that are harmful to the environment (rather than to restrict output *per se*). At the same time, a parallel objective is to encourage firms and individuals to substitute towards more environmentally friendly production activities and consumption goods. To the extent that firms are able to adjust technologies to avoid the tax, market share and domestic jobs in the industry may be restored.

Another positive impact to remember is that where a given product or service can no longer be profitably produced as a result of a green tax reform, other sectors of the economy producing near substitutes would be expected to enjoy increased demand for their output. Thus job losses, income reductions and tax revenue losses that would generally accompany the decline of the targeted group of firms could be offset at least in part (and perhaps more) by increased demand in other sectors of the economy.

4.2.1. *Broader Impacts on the Economy*

A carbon tax, having the intended effect of reducing energy-intensive outputs (*e.g.*, steel production), would through this direct effect lead to a reduction in GDP. However, it is not clear that in each case a carbon tax would lower the productivity growth of the country, which many economists take to be the best measure of a country's overall international competitiveness. In fact there exists evidence, from the application of environmental regulation, that a better environment may not conflict with improved competitiveness.[7]

In some cases, environmental constraints may produce positive effects on economic competitiveness because of the effects that it has on the research and development (R&D) behaviour of firms. Shifts in the direction and timing of technical change, accompanied by changes of production processes and by increasing returns of scale, could break the negative link between growth and environment. Innovations, both of clean products and of end-of-pipe or clean equipment, may in some cases improve the competitiveness of firms. Environmental policies can generate new opportunities and even strengthen the competitive situation in countries that are the first to innovate in this area. It is possible that environmental policy constraints induce innovative responses which more than offset the cost increase and so are favourable to the long-term profitability and growth. This implies that an initial shock in energy prices may be beneficial, in the long term, to the economy and could lock in a new industry and thereby enhance competitiveness. Italy provides an example of this: the increased share in export-production of small vehicles with a low fuel consumption engine that was designed in a response to the high rates of tax on fuel.[8]

The impact of a carbon tax on competitiveness at the country level would depend in part on the impact of the tax at the level of the firm/industry, considered above. At the same time, influencing factors operate in more diverse, complex ways. For example, positive impacts would be felt to the extent that the tax revenues were recycled to lower factor prices of firms outside the hardest hit industries, or to reduce fiscal deficits, partially alleviating pressure to increase taxes in other areas. These indirect effects could partly offset the reduction in output and income in energy-intensive sectors. However, these positive effects would depend on the tax structure, fiscal position and structure of the economy including the energy and labour intensity of key sectors, and on the exact form of the revenue recycling, and may materialise only in the short to medium term, should environmentally related tax revenues and revenue recycling decline along with fossil fuel consumption.

A number of further indirect effects would also be important to assessing the overall impact on international competitiveness. For example, a reduction in the domestic supply of energy-intensive goods (*e.g.*, steel) could mean increased factor costs to industries using those goods as intermediate inputs (*e.g.*, automobile manufacturers). In particular, where a reduction in domestic supply requires increased imports priced to include transportation costs, the average and marginal costs of the consuming industry could be increased. In other words, higher costs could be incurred in other markets.

At the same time, other sectors and countries could benefit. For example, R&D undertaken to adopt technologies to avoid the carbon tax could generate spillover benefits to other producers and sectors. This spillover effect is particularly attractive from a global view, as it could lower the cost to developing countries of accessing technologies and production processes that are less damaging to the environment.

4.2.2. *Empirical studies of the impact of carbon taxes*

A study by Baron and ECON-Energy (1996) looks at the potential impact of a carbon tax, using a statistical survey of industrial structures considering energy (and carbon) intensity and of the structure of international trade in OECD and non-OECD countries. The study shows that high carbon intensity tends to follow high energy intensity, but with differences between different OECD regions. The highest energy and carbon intensity values are observed in Australia, Canada and the United States.

The greater the carbon intensity of an industrial sector, the more pronounced will be the impact of a carbon tax on sectoral competitiveness. There are other structural factors that need to be taken into account, however, such as the position of industries on the world market and the structure of production and trade in different countries or regions. In the OECD area, energy intensive industries were found to contribute between roughly 20% to 25% of GDP. The proportion of exports consisting of energy intensive products is also shown to vary considerably according to region and country: while only 15% of total OECD/Europe energy intensive products are exported to countries other than Annex I,[9] the proportion is greater than 30% for North America, and almost 70% for OECD/Pacific countries. Discrepancies are found for imports as well: energy intensive products (iron and steel, non-ferrous metals, pulp and paper, chemical products) account for only a relatively modest proportion of total trade (between 3.2% and 7.5% of exports and between 1% and 3.7% of imports).

Baron and ECON-Energy have calculated the cost increases from a US$100 per tonne of carbon tax on energy intensive industries. The results indicate a cost increase varying between 1.2% and 5.2% by country, with further variations according to sectors (see Table 3).

Cost increases are generally low (less than 2%), except for Australia, Canada, and the United States, which have more carbon intensive economies than average. In fact, the lower the energy (and carbon) intensity, the weaker the impact of a carbon tax on competitiveness; its impact would therefore probably be limited in Japan and the European Union. On the other hand, more marked short-term effects might be expected in other countries, such as Australia and Canada. In the longer-term these countries have the largest scope to fuel-switch. There are also marked differences in the cost impact of the hypothetical carbon tax by industry sector within countries, clearly indicating the probable net taxpaying sectors under such a tax (those sectors with the highest values). It should be noted that this is a *static* analysis, which does not take account of the tax implications for the economy as a whole and its effects on prices in general. This analysis shows that even co-ordinated implementation of energy/carbon taxes will have differential welfare impacts between countries because of differences in carbon and energy intensity.

Table 3. **Selected OECD countries cost increases[1] from a tax of US$100/ton carbon**
In per cent of production value

	Total energy-intensive industries	Iron and steel	Non-Ferrous metals	Chemical	Pulp and paper
USA	2.8 (2.5)	2.3	3.1	2.8 (2.2)	3.2
Canada	4.1 (3.3)	6.2	3.7	4.1 (2.3)	5.0
Japan	1.2 (1.0)	2.0	0.7	1.0 (0.6)	0.6
Australia	5.2 (5.0)	5.8	11.4	1.7 (1.4)	2.6
France	1.4 (1.1)	2.4	1.4	1.3 (0.8)	0.6
Germany	1.6 (1.4)	2.6	1.2	1.4 (1.1)	1.0
United Kingdom	1.6 (1.3)	3.6	1.9	1.2 (0.8)	1.2
Italy	1.4 (1.2)	2.0	1.1	1.3 (0.9)	0.7
Belgium	2.3 (2.1)	7.3	40.8	1.6 (1.2)	0.6

1. The figures also include carbon emissions through electricity generation and from process emissions in aluminium production. Numbers in parentheses indicate cost increases when the tax is applied only to fossil fuels used for energy purposes, *i.e.* not-sequestered in the final products
Source: OECD/IEA data, ECON-Energy calculations.

An interesting country study by Honkatukia (2000) considers the impact across sectors of a hypothetical doubling in current Finish carbon taxes, under the assumption that tax revenues are recycled via a cut in employers' social security contributions. The work analyses the net impact of higher environmentally related taxation on each sector under two alternative scenarios: one where the supplementary carbon tax is levied only on fuels and one where the supplementary carbon tax is also levied on electricity (see Table 4).

The results show that the supplementary tax on fuels raises net taxes for the paper and transport sectors whilst the electrical and electronics industry and the private service sector gain. Under the supplementary carbon taxes on both fuels and electricity scenario the paper and heavy metals industries are considerable net tax payers, whilst the impact on the transport sector is lower than under the fuel only supplement.

Analysis of the German ecological tax reform concludes that as a result of numerous exemptions and rebates most industry sectors face an additional tax burden of less than 1% of turnover. Furthermore for most sectors the compensation, resulting from lower contributions to pension schemes,

Table 4. **Changes in tax revenue by sector in Finland in 2010**

%

Sector	Supplementary tax on fuels	Supplementary tax on fuels and electricity
Paper industry	7.3	32.9
Heavy metals industry	−0.4	14.2
Electrical and electronics industry	−3.3	−5.3
Transportation	3.3	1.0
Private service	−2.7	−3.4

Source: Honkatukia (2000).

outweighs higher taxation. Only agriculture and the retail and transport sectors face a strongly negative balance.

4.3. Evidence of competitiveness impacts and current mitigation practices

As noted above, generally those industries that in principle would be expected to pay the largest share of environmentally related taxes imposed on business have been very successful in obtaining rebates and exemptions from these levies on account of competitiveness concerns. This fact makes it obviously difficult to assess the hypothetical question of what the impact would have been, had the competitiveness claims been ignored. As noted below, where the competitiveness issue has been assessed, generally the findings have been that competition has not been significantly negatively affected for one or more reasons, including lobbying efforts and careful drafting of the tax laws so as to exempt those that would be hardest hit. Certain distortions have been identified, however, across industries and regions on account of the non-uniform application of environmental taxes.

In particular, there are some recent studies that show some negative impact of environmentally related taxes on *regional* competitiveness. For example, the Norwegian electricity tax has been shown to not only have distorted competition between all other industries and the manufacturing industry that does not pay the tax, but also between southern and northern parts of Norway, Finnmark and the north of Troms, which are exempt from the tax. An assessment of proposed higher carbon taxes in Finland arrived at similar conclusions. These results demonstrate that competing firms have different initial cost structures and abatement costs resulting from different specific carbon intensities, substitution possibilities, and perhaps regulations (Baranzini *et al.*, 2000). Competitive losses/advantages result from these different specific circumstances.

An *ex post* study undertaken by Ecotec investigates the distributional and competitive impacts of the UK landfill tax. While there was concern that the tax would distribute the tax burden to sectors producing large quantities of waste, the report found little evidence of a significant distributional or competitive effect, in part because the tax represents a small proportion of production costs for businesses and because of the rebates and exemptions applied.

Jaffe *et al.* (1995) examine over 100 studies on the potential effect of environmental regulations (thus not only taxes) on the competitiveness of American industry and find that "Overall, there is relatively little evidence to support the hypothesis that environmental regulations have had a large adverse effect on competitiveness, however that elusive term is defined". A key reason of course for this finding is that, generally speaking, environmental protection costs that have been imposed have been relatively modest, too low to affect competitiveness. Other contributing factors identified were comparable environmental constraints across OECD countries (which is not necessarily the case in other regions of the world), and the fact that when environmental constraints are less restrictive in a given country, it tends to be the case that outside investors apply stricter standards than those of the host country.

A review of current green tax policies in OECD countries shows a wide array of measures in place to address in part perceived competitiveness problems. The main measures are summarised below (see also Box 10 above).

4.3.1. *Reduced tax rates, exemptions and tax ceilings*

Many countries apply reduced tax rates for industry. For instance, Sweden initially gave industry a 75% rebate on the carbon tax (and total exemption in the case of the energy tax), meaning that only 25% of the basic carbon tax rate was applied.[10] The rebate was then reduced to 50% in July 1997. In Denmark, a 50% rebate on the CO_2 tax was granted to industry for the period 1993-1995. Both cases are interesting cases of "front runners", who were amongst the first set of countries to introduce CO_2 taxes.

More recently Germany introduced a 20% rebate on electricity taxes for the production sector, while the UK has an 80% rebate on its energy tax (on condition that energy-intensive users sign up to binding energy efficiency negotiated agreements). Most OECD countries have introduced a differentiated CO_2/energy tax system that imposes the lowest rates (or a zero rate) on the most energy-intensive industries, but with some incentives to gradually change the fuel mix towards lower carbon-content.

In many other cases, full tax exemptions are granted for specific activities, sectors or products related to environment related taxes. The OECD database shows around 1 000 exemptions for 235 identified environmentally related taxes. In some cases the exemptions are granted to address certain social, environmental and economic reasons, and therefore only a proportion of these exemptions can be construed as motivated by competitiveness concerns. One approach in granting exemptions is to exclude the main industries from the application of the tax. For example, the new Dutch regulatory tax on energy applies exclusively to households and small businesses. Another approach is to exempt the energy products used mainly by heavy industry: most countries do not tax coal and coke at all, while the few countries that have taxes on these products grant very significant exemptions.

Finally, note that exemptions may be conditional (sometimes referred to as *tax conditionality*). In such cases, an environmental tax is applied only if industry does not achieve predefined objectives or commitments. For instance, in Switzerland, the CO_2 bill provides for a "subsidiary tax" on carbon if industry fails to attain emission abatement objectives via voluntary agreements. In Denmark, concessions on the CO_2 tax are granted to industries which have entered a negotiated agreement with the government to cut emissions.

Effective tax rates may also be kept down by introducing tax ceilings or limits on the amount of tax paid. Tax ceilings are used in Austria, Finland, Germany and Sweden to protect particular sectors from high taxes. For example, in Germany if charges exceed DM 1 000 per year (or over 50 MWh electricity) enterprises in manufacturing, agriculture and forestry pay only 20% of the standard rate on electricity and of the tax increase for heating oil and gas. Second, if tax payments exceed by 20% the savings made by reduced contributions to the pension insurance, employers can claim a refund.

4.3.2. *Tax refunds*

The OECD/EU database records 25 cases of refunds for certain business sectors or activities. For example, Denmark's carbon tax structure grants a variety of refunds to industry. Here again, it is difficult to ascertain whether refunds are specifically designed to reduce possible competitiveness effects. However, while a few refunds aim at "rewarding" environment-friendly practices or processes, most are designed to lighten the tax burden of industry, under specific conditions.

4.3.3. *Recycling*

Recycling tax revenue is yet another way to address perceived competitiveness concerns, as discussed in Chapter 1.6.2. In Denmark, for example, CO_2 and SO_2 taxes are fully redistributed to industry in the form of lower employers' social security contributions and subsidies for energy saving investments.

4.3.4. Gradual implementation (phase-in)

Gradual phasing-in of taxes can soften the immediate cost impact, while giving companies time to plan for production adjustments to avoid the tax. The German electricity tax was introduced at a rate of DM 20 per MWh, and is increased by DM5 per MWh annually in the period 2000-2003. The German mineral oil duties are also set to rise annually by set amounts over the same period.[11] Finland phased-in the effects of its electricity tax by phasing out the initial rebate. In particular, manufacturing industry in Finland initially paid just 54% of the electricity tax, rising to 61% in 1998.

4.3.5. Border tax adjustments

Border tax adjustments (BTAs) can be usefully applied to address competitiveness concerns in certain markets. Imposing a tax on imports of targeted goods can help protect domestic producers of those goods from foreign competition. However, levying tax on goods produced domestically or imported raises competitiveness concerns where those goods are used further along production chains. In particular, it can make exports of these later-stage products more difficult, and imports more attractive. Moreover import or export BTAs tend to be imprecise and distorting, at least in certain cases. For example, imposing an import tax on imported steel in respect of the amount of coal that has been used in its production abroad is difficult. Generally, the same is true whenever attempting to tax a product that is embedded or used in the production of a given import. Similarly, measurement and administration problems can be encountered when providing relief to exports of steel in respect of the amount of carbon tax embedded in the pre-adjustment export price. An approximate approach could be unfair and distorting if different production technologies are used by different producers, in different countries, and over time, implying a varying coal content. Thus the administrative and compliance costs with establishing the correct BTA could be large. Largely for these reasons, WTO rulings may not be favourable in respect of BTAs determined on the basis of imputed inputs, both in the case of import and export adjustments.

An example of a BTA in practice is the tax levied by the US on imported products containing ozone depleting substances (ODS), but also on products where such substances are believed to have been used in the production process – even if they are no longer contained in the product. To calculate the tax, the ODS weight of an imported product is estimated using US standard production data and the tax rates listed in Table A3.1. Importers that can prove that the ODS weight of their products is below these benchmarks, are taxed at a lower rate. Where it is difficult to calculate the ODS weight of a product, a value method is used, whereby the tax is equivalent to 1% of the product value.

4.4. The impact and costs of mitigation measures

While the existing array of mitigation measures may be judged in a country's best interest in certain cases, it is important to assess the possible *longer-term* impacts of the current design of most energy, CO_2 and other environmentally related taxes. First, the design of taxes (revenue recycling mechanisms and exemptions) impacts on the development of new technologies and/or the development of the industrial structure of the country in question. Exemptions tend to "lock in" energy/carbon-intensive or otherwise polluting processes and thus perpetuate harmful effects on the economy. The negative environmental impacts of exemptions and rebates will in many cases be highly problematic as the sectors given special treatment tend to be the largest polluters.

Second, in order to meet pre-determined emission reduction targets such as those set under the Kyoto protocol, greater abatement would be required from sectors paying the tax. As greater abatement generally involves higher abatement costs at the margin, this means that such an outcome would entail higher overall abatement costs and thus an inefficient and sub-optimal transition path in meeting obligations to pollute less. In addition to these efficiency concerns, these higher costs of abatement would tend to place such firms at a greater cost disadvantage, raising not only business competitiveness concerns in these areas, but also fairness in the application of the tax system.

Böhringer and Rutherford (1997) investigated the costs of exemptions and rebates of a hypothetical carbon tax in Germany. Exemptions were based on government proposals to provide relief to those sectors where energy costs form more than 3.75% of total production costs or where exports form more than 15% of total turnover. These "rules" effectively exempt chemical, ceramic, glass, iron and steel, non-ferrous metals, casting and paper sectors from taxation. In 1990 these sectors accounted for 8% of gross output, 6% of employment and 12% of carbon emissions. These potentially exempted sectors are significantly more carbon-intensive, *i.e.* the ratio of carbon emissions to output is higher than in other sectors subject to the tax. There are two conclusions to be drawn: first the exempted sectors have more opportunities for CO_2-substitution than other sectors and second their exclusion from taxation means other sectors with less scope for (and more costly) carbon reduction will face higher tax rates and will have to achieve greater emissions cuts. Therefore the pattern of carbon reduction undertaken to achieve set emission reduction targets will be inefficient, as many low-cost energy savings/CO_2 emission reductions options available in the energy-intensive sectors will fall outside the scope of the tax.

Böhringer and Rutherford (1997) find that the potential exemptions would have raised the total costs of emission abatement of achieving a 30% reduction in carbon emissions from the 1990 level by around a fifth. Furthermore they find that an alternative policy combining a uniform carbon tax and wage subsidies targeted to the potentially exempted sectors not only retains more jobs but is less costly than the tax exemption policy. They conclude that "*targeted instruments* (carbon taxes together with wage subsidies) are clearly superior to *blunt instruments* (a CO_2 tax with exemptions)". These results and conclusions are based on the assumption that carbon leakage rates are low. If however leakage rates (relocation of emissions to other countries) are high then partial tax exemptions might increase efficiency of global CO_2 reduction (Böhringer *et al.*, 1997). Therefore it is important to estimate leakage rates for efficient design of unilateral abatement policy.

A third point, with certain industry sectors or activities subject to environmental taxes at given rates, and others not, and with the prospect of higher abatement demands placed on these targeted areas, more capital might flow to the exempt group. Uncertainty over possibly higher future abatement costs in the targeted group would be perceived as a source of risk by investors who would demand a premium on expected rates of return on equity to compensate for this additional risk. Higher costs of capital would further increase business costs for the targeted sector, and might be expected to result in capital flowing to the non-targeted sector. Thus in the end such a policy could lead to more as opposed to less investment in the most heavily polluting sectors, and thus greater environmental damage globally.

Fourth, the competitiveness of an economy could be placed under a greater threat if industry sectors are protected and steps are not taken today to adjust early to cleaner production technologies. Where serious environmental damage assessments in the future lead to necessary and dramatic changes in business activity, the costs of making the adjustment will be much higher if the transition is delayed. This follows from the fact that abatement costs tend to rise at the margin so that the greater is the level of abatement required in any period, the greater is the overall abatement cost. In other words, an ill-prepared and radical adjustment would entail huge costs on not only the environment, but also on the structure of the domestic economy over the longer term.

Fifth, and related to the lock-in effect already noted, measures that minimise the application of environmental taxes lead to little R&D in new, less environmentally damaging production technologies. More R&D would over time lead to lower-cost means of achieving given pollution abatement. A very important element of a global strategy to reduce environmental damage, including global warming, is to include as many countries as possible towards this end. This is obviously more difficult in developing countries, which feel that they should not be denied the use of relatively cheap production methods to get them to the stage of economic development that larger countries, including OECD countries, now enjoy. However, by encouraging R&D, more environmentally friendly technologies can be made available to these countries at a lower cost.

Sixth, an issue discussed further below, is whether competitiveness concerns and the harmful effects of existing mitigation measures can be addressed by a co-ordinated effort among OECD Member countries to move together towards a sustainable development path.

In addressing the competitiveness issue, it is useful to ask whether governments have responded too quickly to the loss-of-competitiveness arguments from industry, and whether more might be done.

As noted, the cost impact of a carbon or energy tax can be reduced either by switching to lower-carbon fuels, reducing energy use overall (energy-efficiency measures), or reducing or changing production. Governments respond to industry claims that the cost will come in terms of reduced production. However it is exactly these sub-sectors that will have the greatest scope (and incentives) for switching to lower carbon fuels and for energy efficiency investments with the imposition of a tax. The scope for fuel switching and energy efficiency by industry sector and country has in most cases not been tested.

Governments may still introduce rebates and exemptions to reduce the short-term negative competitive impacts and thereafter follow a policy of phasing-in tax rate increases (*e.g.* German ecological taxes) or phasing-out tax rebates/exemptions (*e.g.* Finland's electricity tax rebates to industry). Such temporary relief would provide a cushion to industry but still provide a clear, environmentally determined price signal for fuel switching, energy efficiency investments, and longer-term industrial restructuring. There will be losers in such economic restructuring; unprofitable carbon-intensive sectors will either be phased out or made more efficient, and other, often more labour-intensive sectors could experience rapid development. Furthermore, the impact of revenue recycling, including through cuts in labour or capital taxation, targeted labour subsidies, or linking rebates with the energy intensity (or some other measure of environmental efficiency) of production, could be investigated.[12]

4.5. Possible responses to the competitiveness issue – a case for tax co-ordination?

The OECD/EU database on environmentally related taxes records numerous exemptions and rebates for many taxes, reducing the coverage and environmental effectiveness of taxes. Further, one can speculate how competitiveness would be affected if carbon taxes were introduced at the sort of levels required to attain the objectives of the United Nation's Convention on Climate Change, and more specifically, those of the Kyoto Protocol.

As examined in Section 4.2, a carbon tax that significantly increases the cost of fossil fuel consumption, if implemented unilaterally, would be expected to lead to a loss of sales, a loss of market share, and plant closures in a number of cases, primarily in sectors where fossil fuels are a main cost component. While generally all sectors relying on fossil fuels to some extent would be affected, including those using fuels only to heat plant or office space or those relying on transportation services, the most pronounced effects would be felt on energy-intensive firms and industries.[13] However, identifying in hard numbers and facts what the competitive losses would be from unilateral action is difficult, and estimates are largely uncertain. Given this, one possibility worth exploring to address international competitiveness concerns would be international agreement concerning how to implement one or more environmentally related tax.

In the context of the earlier discussion, one could consider as an example the implications of adopting similar rules for the imposition of carbon taxes, levying a similar tax burden on similar industries across participating countries. In principle, under such an agreement, all affected firms would lower their fossil fuel consumption up to the point where the marginal abatement cost equals the chosen carbon tax rate. Assuming a uniform tax rate, marginal abatement costs would be equated across firms and green house gas emissions would be controlled at minimal cost. The results of such a regime would stand in contrast to the results sketched out in 4.2 that consider unilateral adoption of a carbon tax.

In a world increasingly open to foreign trade and competition, firms subject to *unilateral adoption* of a factor tax would not be able to pass the tax on through higher output prices. Output prices in competitive markets can be taken to be more or less fixed, set in international markets and invariant to domestic unilateral decisions to impose a factor tax. As a result, unilateral adoption of a carbon tax would be expected to result in reductions in the profits of domestic firms, and in losses and plant closures in the more competitive output markets.

In contrast, with *co-ordinated implementation* where all firms in a given industry regardless of the country of production face the same uniform carbon tax, implying a common cost element across countries, one would observe an increase in the world price of energy-intensive products. In this case, the burden of the tax would not fall on domestic producers, consumers and labour alone. With higher prices, international demand for the product would fall, but the burden of the tax would be shared across a broader base (for an elaboration, see Annex II).

While attractive perhaps in theory, a number of potential difficulties may be identified with attempts to obtain an international agreement on co-ordinated implementation of a carbon tax. First, countries would differ in terms of the taxes/charges in place prior to the introduction of a new carbon tax that affect the cost of fossil fuels. Thus, the imposition of a carbon tax at a uniform rate would mean unequal fossil fuel tax rates on similar industries across participating countries. With unequal fossil fuel tax rates, marginal abatement costs in a given industry would vary across countries, implying an inefficient outcome. Eliminating existing taxes on fossil fuels to address this problem seems unrealistic where the taxes are introduced for non-environmental reasons (*e.g.*, raising revenue), or where the revenues are earmarked to finance certain public programs, or where the taxes are imposed by sub-central levels of government not party to the agreement. Introducing a carbon tax at a non-uniform rate – with country-specific rates conditional on existing tax rates on fossil fuels (*e.g.*, chosen to give a uniform combined tax rate on fossil fuel consumption) – could also be difficult, as disagreements would likely ensue over the list of taxes to be included in the list, and the effective tax rates.

Second, the adoption of a uniform rate (set with or without regard to other existing fossil fuel taxes) would impose different total abatement costs on different countries. In particular, certain countries with significant energy-intensive sectors and little progress made in moving towards improved technologies or away from polluting sectors would be particularly hard hit. These countries would likely argue that they require special transitional relief, including for example delayed or phased-in implementation and perhaps discretionary financial relief to compensate their economy from the negative consequences stemming from significant competitiveness concerns.

Despite these difficulties, concerted approached to the practical design of carbon taxes, and perhaps other environmentally related taxes, holds considerable appeal. Such an approach offers a response to those arguing against the introduction of environmentally related taxes on international competitiveness grounds. At the same time, considerable peer pressure can be brought to bear on countries to implement green tax reform, if other countries appear willing to move in this direction.

To take an example, a 1998 study by the Centre for Energy Conservation and Environment Technology (the Netherlands) considers a pan-European approach to address aviation-related CO_2 and NO_x emissions.[14] The study presents convincing arguments for the application of economic instruments applied across Europe, favouring an emissions tax over a fuel tax. In part, the attractiveness of the former is that it is unlikely to raise legal obstacles (the report notes that contrary to popular perception, an emissions charge would not be in conflict with the Chicago Convention or with bilateral Air Service Agreements). While a fuel charge may be easier to implement, the report details how an emissions charge could work based on an internationally accepted method to calculate emissions. Finally, the report identifies problems encountered when the policy strategy is limited to European countries, which leads to a call for an assessment of the net benefits within the context of broader international participation.

4.6. Conclusions

Dealing with international competitiveness concerns raises a number of difficult and complex issues that encourage policy-makers to rethink choices over appropriate environmental tax-bases, tax rates and exemptions. In certain situations, competitiveness arguments do not hold and environmentally related taxes can be introduced unilaterally and without extensive rebates and exemptions, in particular where the taxed item is not widely traded (*e.g.*, landfill and wastewater taxes). Even in those sectors where international trade is a factor, unilateral action can proceed where feasible options are available to affected firms to reduce their tax burden, for example by fuel switching in response to a carbon tax or investing in abatement technology and clean product/production development. Too often in such cases these responses are delayed by the granting of rebates and exemptions, or not introducing environmentally related taxes or similar policy measures in the first place. Phasing out rebates and exemptions and pre-announcing the introduction of new environmentally related taxes and tax rate increases are two policy options that would improve the environmental effectiveness of environmentally related taxation in such instances.

Where unilateral action is taken, consideration might be given to a dual (two-tier) rate structure, with a lower rate for the more internationally exposed sectors. Furthermore, countries examining revenue recycling as an option should consider imposing environmental taxes on industry while introducing innovative methods to channel part of the environmental tax revenues back to industry in such a way that marginal abatement incentives are not reduced. Countries should also explore how environmentally motivated tax reform can best be integrated with broader fiscal reforms, given that it is the combined effects of the tax system and reform measures that determines the effect of host country taxation on competitiveness.

Despite clear cases for unilateral action, unilateral efforts can be frustrated where environmental taxes can be avoided due to varying treatment across jurisdictions (*e.g.*, where higher environmental fuel taxes can be avoided through increased cross-border fuel shopping). Increased co-operation in such areas could go a long way towards minimising scope for avoidance. Moreover, in making a case for unilateral action, sorting out when competitiveness arguments hold, and when they do not, is often difficult. This stems from the general uncertainty over behavioural responses to new environmental taxes, including the possible out-migration of firms to jurisdictions with a more lenient policy approach. Moreover, acceptance building is particularly elusive where significant job losses may result and when it is recognised that output reductions or fundamental changes in technologies used are an intended policy outcome, at least in certain sectors.

The fallout from an ambitious environmental program, including the social costs incurred while an economy adjusts away from harmful environmental practices, often makes imperative a search for ways to minimise these negative effects. However, finding the right balance to competing objectives is rarely an straight-forward task. Protecting against output contractions by under-pricing environmental damages, for example by setting environmentally related tax rates low, providing generous exemptions, or focusing on "end-of-pipe" solutions alone, can increase overall costs in meeting environmental goals. This may be particularly true when viewed over the longer run, factoring in the welfare of future generations. While announcements and a phasing-in of implementation can be usefully applied to prepare for environmental reform, many would contend that too often such announcements are not followed through with serious measures that adequately account for environmental damages tied to currently harmful economic activities.

As noted, border tax adjustments (BTAs) can be usefully applied to address competitiveness concerns in certain markets. However, even where BTA protection is possible for a given industry, this does not ensure protection for the domestic economy further along production chains where application of BTAs is more difficult. In particular, technical, administrative and legal constraints may apply in using BTAs, implying that such mechanisms cannot be relied upon in each instance to adequately protect the sectors in question from competitiveness pressures.

These various shortcomings with unilateral approaches in certain cases raise the prospect of considering a co-ordinated approach. The environmental effectiveness of a regionally or internationally co-ordinated environmentally related tax could offer environmental benefits through reducing the pressures for exemptions and border tax adjustments. While such co-ordination remains an aspiration, gradual efforts in this direction should be taken. Countries should be encouraged to share information, experiences and best practices concerning options and opportunities for using environmental taxes and similar instruments to address common environmental concerns. For example, one option that would appear to deserve greater attention is for co-ordinated implementation of an environmental (emissions-based) aviation tax. Additional research should also be undertaken and shared that analyses the combined implementation of taxes and other approaches (tradable permits, voluntary agreements, etc.) by different countries in the pursuit of environmental goals. Countries concerned with competitiveness implications of adjusting certain environmentally related taxes on a unilateral basis may also wish to consider possible concerted policy options and changes, decided and implemented at the national level, but within a framework which provides for a multilateral dialogue.

NOTES

1. Most OECD countries do not tax, or tax only at low rates, coal, coke, and heavy fuel oil used primarily by industry. In some countries agriculture is also protected from high taxes. For example, the Netherlands offers rebates from its energy taxes to horticulture. However, this sector is part of the agro-industry environmental agreement. The objective of this agreement is to increase energy efficiency by 50% between 1980 and 2000. In the UK intensive pig and poultry rearing are eligible for an 80% discount, with a negotiated agreement, from the tax on business and industry energy use, and horticulture is entitled to a temporary 50% discount. All other agriculture pays full levy rates.

2. The number of instances where one or a small number of domestic firms are able to exercise market power and increase output prices to cover carbon tax imposed at significant rates generally would be limited in most OECD Member-countries. The relevant sectors would include those protected by tariff and/or non-tariff barriers, and industrial sectors consisting of firms (with heavy reliance on fossil fuels as a factor component) having exclusive rights to rent-producing assets (*e.g.*, natural resources).

3. Note that economic profit refers to profit over and above the amount required to attract share capital.

4. The price mechanism of the carbon tax provides incentives for R&D in pollution abatement, as firms search for cost-effective ways of production to achieve emission and tax reductions, leading to more energy efficient technologies. Such incentives are likely to be greater the more competitive the industry (*i.e.*, the scarcer the existence of economic rents). Note that a positive amount of carbon tax would be expected in the long run (assuming less than full abatement), as under a carbon tax polluters pay a tax on remaining emissions from their use of fossil fuels.

5. A range of factors in addition to environmental taxes impact on the competitiveness of firms. A partial list of other tax considerations would include effective tax rates on other factors (social security taxes, payroll taxes, property taxes), income taxes, withholding taxes on distributions/payments, and the final incidence of these taxes. Similarly, there are many important location-specific cost considerations unrelated to tax that need to be taken into account, such as proximity to input and output markets, access to skilled labour, infrastructure, legal/regulatory structure.

6. This implies that the maximum carbon tax rate that could avoid plant closures would therefore depend on the initial relative cost advantages enjoyed by the sector. Another point to recall is that the impact of a carbon tax on after-tax production costs depends on the use of the carbon tax revenues. To the extent that the revenues are used to reduce labour or capital taxes paid by the firms most affected by the tax, then the impact of the tax on total costs would be lessened (as generally would be the incentive to adjust away from the tax-base).

7. Environmental regulations in the US have not reduced US productivity growth. See Repetto and Austin (1997).

8. For details, see: Carraro and Siniscalco (1996), Osculati (1997) and Porter and van der Linde (1995).

9. Annex I Parties to the United Nations Framework Convention on Climate Change (FCCC) are the industrialised countries (Most OECD Member-countries plus nine non-OECD countries at the time of the agreement in 1992).

10. A rebate at rate R means that the effective rate of tax is given by $t(1-R)$, where t is the basic rate of the given environmental tax. Note that – in principle – a tax rebate differs from a tax refund in that with a tax refund, the basic or full amount of tax is paid, and then some percentage of that amount is given back to the taxpayers. In contrast, under a rebate mechanism, the tax relief is immediately applied (*i.e.*, only the reduced amount of tax is paid). However, in this report, a clear distinction between the two is not always made.

11. The mineral oil duty on motor fuels will rise by 0.06 DM per litre per year.

12. Implementing subsidy policies requires compliance with European Union and WTO state aid rules.

13. Economic analyses of the effects of a carbon tax tend to focus on the hardest hit sectors, while recognising that similar, but less pronounced, effects could be felt more generally across other consuming sectors.

14. See Centre for Energy Conservation and Environmental Technology (1998). For a fuller discussion of issues related to taxation of aviation, see also EEA (2000).

Chapter 5

THE INCOME DISTRIBUTION ISSUE

5.1. Available evidence on income distribution impacts

5.1.1. Energy/carbon taxation

Evidence on the distributive implications of environmentally related taxes remains mixed and limited. There is some evidence that energy taxes tend to be income regressive, however the degree of income regressivity in many cases is weak [Barde (1997) and OECD (1997)]. Empirical results show that energy taxation is income regressive in Denmark, Ireland and the UK, whereas, it is found to be income progressive in Spain and Italy [Symons and Proop (1998)]. Barker and Köhler (1998) tested the income distribution impacts of different energy taxes, using data from eleven EU countries. They found that the distributional impact of energy/carbon taxes differs by energy use. For example, taxation of transport fuels is weakly progressive, whilst taxation of domestic energy has a weakly regressive impact. Overall they conclude that energy/carbon taxation is weakly regressive, because the domestic energy impact dominates the transport fuel impact.

Other country assessments of the equity impact of carbon taxes conclude that taxes are weakly regressive. In its 1997 report, the Swedish Green Tax Commission estimated that doubling the CO_2 tax (from a 1997 rate of SEK 0.37 to SEK 0.74 per kg of CO_2) would have a weak regressive impact. The report concluded that the lowest income group would need to receive compensation of 1.24% of their consumption expenditure, in order to maintain the same consumption level, compared to 0.78% for the highest income group. In a similar study, Honkatukia (2000) investigated the income distribution impact of a supplementary FIM100 per tonne of CO_2 tax (raising the tax to FIM200 per tonne of CO_2), and that for current taxes on traffic fuels. The results of the study showed that both the higher CO_2 tax, and the current taxes on traffic fuels, are regressive, particularly on the lowest income group. The report concluded that the lowest income group would need to receive compensation of 1.96% of their consumption expenditure in order to maintain the same consumption level, compared to 0.89% for the highest income group . In addition, it was found that increased CO_2 taxation widened income differentials between regions, with sparsely populated regions bearing the heaviest tax burden.

The German tax reform has been calculated to benefit most households, however households with children will benefit the most [RWI (1999)]. If induced employment effects of the reform are taken into account, the picture looks especially good, since the reform is expected to improve the situation of the unemployed, in particular. For those in receipt of a pension, the disadvantage will only be temporal, since pensions are automatically adjusted according to the development of net incomes in general. Low-income households receiving social assistance can claim higher allowances for increased heating costs. In addition, it should be mentioned that, on social grounds, electricity used in night storage heaters installed before the 1st April 1999 is taxed at only half rate. Overall, the distributional incidence of the reform package will depend thus primarily on the employment effects induced by the reform. Their magnitude depends crucially on the outcome of wage negotiations. If they neutralise the incentive effects, no additional jobs will be created. Model calculations suggest that over the period 2000-2005 the tax component of the reform would lead to a loss of 17 000 jobs per year, while the reduction in labour costs would result in 93 000 additional jobs per year, resulting in an overall increase of about 75 000 jobs. This study highlights the importance of other aspects – such as compensation, employment effects and the distribution of environmental benefit – in determining the distributional impacts of a tax reform (see Section 1.7.2).

Metcalf (1998) studied the income distribution impacts of a hypothetical tax reform package in the US. The reform package combined a $40 per tonne carbon tax, higher motor fuel excise, waste taxes and taxes on SO_2, NO_x, PM-10 and VOCs emissions, which together increased government revenue by 10%. In his model, revenue was recycled back to taxpayers through lower marginal rates for income tax and social security contributions; the tax package was *revenue* neutral. The impact of this tax reform was found to be quite regressive. Metcalf investigated ways to make the tax reform *distibutionally* neutral. He found that by targeting recycled revenues to low-income groups, the regressivity of the environmental taxes could be offset, and the reform package made somewhat progressive.

In the US, Walls and Hanson (1999) investigated the equity considerations of replacing the current Californian vehicle registration fees, based on vehicle value, with one of three emissions-related (environmental impact related) fees. The three fees are an emissions fee based on annual mileage, a fee based on total emissions, and a fee based on emissions rates. The results show that if annual income is the chosen measure of household income, all three emissions-related fees are income regressive, compared to the current vehicle registration fee system. The fee based on emissions rates is the most regressive. However, when a household lifetime income measure is used instead of annual income, the three emissions-related fees, including the fee based on total emissions (the most environmental effective fee) though still income regressive, are more similar to the current vehicle registration fee system. It is likely that other environmentally related taxes would also be less regressive under a household lifetime income measure. The authors assert that a different mechanism for returning the revenue raised,[1] perhaps through cuts in the marginal rates of taxation, might better offset the income regressive impacts of emissions-related fees.

In many cases the impact of environmentally related taxation is softened by various mitigation and compensation measures. For example, the German energy tax reform and in the Netherlands energy tax relief has been designed to compensate households with average energy consumption with additional measures to target the most vulnerable, energy-dependent households [Vermeeend and van der Vaart (1998)].

Although these studies show that environmentally related energy and CO_2 taxes are somewhat income regressive, the differences are not that large, and it is likely that it would be possible to compensate the lower-income groups.

5.1.2. *Non-carbon/energy taxation*

There have been few studies on the income distribution impacts of environmentally related taxes other than those on carbon, energy and transport.

The taxation of water supply in Denmark was found to be slightly progressive (Clemmesen, 1995). However, the data may underestimate water costs in low-income households, where water costs are often included in the rent.

5.1.3. *The distribution of environmental benefits*

There is little information on the distribution of environmental benefits following an environmental improvement, brought about by the implementation of an environmentally related tax. However, in Germany Luhmann *et al.* (1998) concluded that in Berlin low-income groups are most affected by emissions of all kinds, and therefore these same groups would benefit most form a reduction in emissions. It is likely that similar results would be found in other major cities in OECD countries.

5.2. Policy options

The OECD/EU database on environmentally related taxes indicates that a number of special tax provisions are applied on equity grounds (see Box 10). Two types of corrective measures can be envisaged to reduce any negative distributional impacts of environmentally related taxation: mitigation and compensation (see Section 1.7.2).

Mitigation is an *ex ante* measure to reduce the rates of environmentally related taxes and therefore alleviate the tax burden for specific groups. The Dutch regulatory tax on small energy users has a zero rate band or a tax floor for the first 800 m^3 per year for gas and 800 kWh per year for electricity. However, in 2001 the Dutch plan to replace these tax-free allowances with a fixed tax reduction per electricity connection. Low-income Dutch households are also exempt from municipal waste collection and sewage taxes. The UK government has ruled out increases to environmentally related taxation on domestic consumption of fuel and power because of alleged undesirable distributional effects.[2]

Compensation measures are basically *ex post* and outside the realm of the taxes as such, *i.e.* they do not affect their rate or structure. Tax refunds are a typical compensation measure; for instance, the Swiss taxes on VOC and on the sulphur content of heating oil are refunded to households on a per capita basis. In 2000, Norway raised household electricity taxes by NOK 0.025 per kWh, however two-thirds of the increased revenue will be transferred back to customers through increased standard allowances and minimum allowances in income taxation. The Danish established a committee to investigate the distributional impact of environmentally related taxes, particularly on household electricity consumption, and to recommend compensation measures. This committee advised against a tax floor, as many low-income users are large electricity consumers. They concluded that a fairer compensation mechanism, and one that would retain the incentive effect of the tax, would be via lump sum transfers within the tax and benefits system. In several countries, energy taxes are partly repaid to household and/or business in the form of subsidies for energy saving investments/expenditures.

The distributional incidence of environmental policy measures has become a key issue in the policy debate. The data show that some environmentally related taxes can be weakly income regressive and also increase regional income disparities in some countries. However, the impact of the tax alone is only part of the story, a full assessment would also include the secondary impact of any compensation payments, tax exemptions, induced employment effects, and the distribution of the environmental benefits resulting from the tax. Mitigation measures are not good practice, as they reduce the environmental effectiveness of taxes. In the case of regressivity, governments should seek other, and more direct, measures if low-income households are to be compensated. Such compensation measures can maintain the price signal of the tax (see Section 1.6.2) whilst reducing the impact of the tax on household income. In addition, governments could introduce complementary policies, for example tougher building regulations to improve energy efficiency.

NOTES

1. In the study, revenue is returned through the abolition of the registration fee.
2. The UK government also supports a number of programmes to improve domestic energy-efficiency and energy suppliers have contractual social obligations.

Chapter 6

ADMINISTRATIVE AND COMPLIANCE COSTS

Administrative costs depend on the design of the tax: taxes with differentiated and complex provisions and rebates are likely to be costly to administer. This is relevant, as the database shows that a raft of exemptions and rebates exist for many environmentally related taxes, including taxes on waste, automotive fuels and other energy sources. It should be noted that some conventional measures of administrative efficiency, such as the ratio of tax revenue to administrative costs, may not be appropriate for environmentally related taxes, because revenues will decline if taxes are environmentally effective. By this measure, some of the most environmentally effective taxes, such as the Danish tax on chlorinated solvents, have become less administratively efficient as they – in line with intentions – reduce the size of the tax-base.

6.1. Factors affecting administrative costs

Administrative costs are incurred both by government and by the taxpayers. Several factors may affect administrative costs, in particular:

- the number of different taxes;
- the number and complexity of tax-bases (the OECD/EC database on environmentally related taxes contains more than 400 taxes and charges, and more than 2 100 tax-bases);
- the number of potential tax-payers (a limited number of producers, or a large segment of the population, such as all car owners);
- the number and complexity of specific tax provisions, like exemptions, refunds, tax ceilings etc. (The database specifies more than 1 000 such provisions);
- the amount of revenues involved, as the importance of calculating the taxes correctly will increase with the size of the payments to be made;
- the pre-existence of pollution inventories and relevant administrative registers; and
- the possibility and difficulties for measuring or estimating polluting emissions.

Where it is possible to administer environmentally related taxes through existing structures, associated administrative costs can be constrained. For instance, many energy and transport-related taxes are managed through already well established procedures, and adding an environmental component to the taxes, should not *a priori*, significantly increase administration costs. The pre-existence of administrative registers and/or pollution inventories and measurement equipment to comply with existing regulations reduces the additional costs of administrating a new environmentally related tax. However, the possibility of wasteful overlap between instruments should be carefully monitored.

6.2. Evidence on administrative costs

There is little data on the administrative costs of environmentally related taxes and, according to questionnaire responses obtained in the preparation of this report, very few countries have planned measures to reduce administrative costs.

United Kingdom has estimates of the costs of administering the landfill tax. The tax raises around £350 million per year and administrative costs are estimated to be around £2 million per year. Therefore, the costs as a percentage of revenue collected, are about 0.56%; this is actual slightly less than the costs of collecting VAT (0.63% costs as a percentage of revenue collected in 1998) but more than the costs for excise duties (0.1% in 1998).[1] Other environmentally related taxes, except those with multiple rebates and exemptions, are likely to have similar magnitudes of administrative costs. Furthermore, it is likely that the administrative efficiency of environmentally related taxes measured in this way will improve as tax rates rise, up to a certain extent, depending on demand elasticities. However, many new energy and CO_2 taxes are complicated in their design because of the large number of exemptions, rebates and negotiated agreements applied.

In Denmark it is estimated that the additional administrative cost of the CO_2 tax is around 1-2% of the tax revenue for taxes levied on business. The tax necessitates a split to be made of energy use in a company between space heating, light processes and heavy processes. The cost estimate above does not include the costs of concluding and verifying a large number of associated negotiated agreements. The administrative costs of entering into these agreements are estimated to amount to 5-12% of the expected subsidies for the reduction of the CO_2 tax in 2000. The administrative cost of applying for subsidies are estimated to about 3-9% of the amount of the subsidies. (Larsen, 2000)

The Swiss federal customs bureau estimates that for the 25 tax-bases on mineral oils the administrative costs are 1.5% of revenues. However, the administrative costs of two planned taxes on non-renewable energy (rejected in a September 2000 referendum) were roughly estimated to be around 5% of revenues. These administrative costs would only have applied to the small earmarked fraction (15% of total revenues) that would have been used to support state investments into renewable energy and efficiency enhancement projects.

An example of very high administrative costs compared to the revenues raised is the Belgian product "ecotaxes". The most modest estimate of the administrative costs (costs of enforcement and collection) of these taxes amounted to BEF 66 million per year, more than twenty times the revenues raised. These costs are high mainly because of the large number of conditions for paying, or not paying, the taxes, and low revenues raised.

The administrative costs associated with the Dutch groundwater tax are small.[2] The tax is levied on 44 water companies, who pass it on to their customers water bills, like VAT. Metering is widespread in the Netherlands, thus simplifying the administration of the tax. A similar conclusion has been reached in Denmark in an evaluation of their water supply tax. Administrative costs are also low because the tax has simply been added to the annual water bill of customers, and metering is widespread (in those cases where there is no metering, a standard 170 m^3 water consumption is assumed).

A study by Miranda, Bauer and Aldy (1995) concerning Seattle [quoted in EPA (2001)] found that waste collection times were increased 10% under the city's weight-based charging system for household wastes. However, under the system, the weight of garbage collected has decreased 15%, which partly offsets the increased collection costs.

Another important aspect of administrative cost is comparisons with alternative policy tools. There is little available evidence on such comparative studies, however, the Netherlands introduced its environmentally related tax reform to replace a system of charges, in order to reduce administrative costs and raise revenue more efficiently. Finally, further work is needed to estimate the division of additional costs between taxpayers.

6.3. Policy options

Whilst no firm or general conclusion can be drawn on the cost of administering environmentally related taxes, this issue should be carefully assessed at the design stage of an environmentally related tax. Where possible, to reduce administrative and compliance costs, environmentally related taxes should piggyback on existing tax structures and administrative registers. Taxes that are complex in their structure, with different rates and special provisions for specific agents, and circumstances, are likely to be more costly to both administer for the relevant government departments, and in terms of compliance and administration costs for business. Taxes that are based on easy to measure emissions, or that target a small number of tax payers, are likely to be least costly to administer.

Administrative costs are only one factor determining the overall efficiency of an environmentally related tax, and the comparative efficiency of taxation compared to alternative policy instruments. Although broad tax-bases are preferable as revenue raisers and for their high administrative efficiency, there is still a case for using taxation as a mechanism to change behaviour. For example, the Danish taxes on chlorinated solvents are highly effective, with the tax base and revenues eroding in parallel with the environmental efficiency of the tax.

NOTES

1. See HM *Customs and Excise Board Report* 1998.
2. This section is based on Ecotec (2000).

Chapter 7

ACCEPTANCE BUILDING

7.1. Green Tax Commissions[1]

A number of OECD countries have set up green tax reform commissions or inter-ministerial working-parties to facilitate and co-ordinate the introduction of environmentally related tax reforms. In such commissions there are often representatives of the major affected groups, for instance from industry and public, academics, and tax and environment experts. The broad nature of such commissions lends them public legitimacy and support. The remit of individual commissions varies, but often include:

- making an inventory of possible environmentally related taxes and charges, and analysing their implications with regard to the economy, the environment, and public administration;
- examining possible ways of utilising the revenues from environmentally related taxes, including the provision of incentives for environmental improvement, or to reduce social security contributions;
- making an inventory of government subsidies that may have a detrimental effect on the environment; and
- investigating possible negative environmental effects from other elements of the fiscal system.

Green tax commissions provide a forum for discussing all aspects of environmentally related taxation, including various mitigation and compensation measures for industry and households, and may help accelerate the introduction of, and political commitment to, environmentally related taxation through involving all major stakeholders in the process of policy formulation.

7.1.1. *The experience with Green Tax Commissions in OECD countries*

Most green tax commissions investigate the difficult issues of competitiveness, income distribution, and the environmental effectiveness of environmentally related taxation, including through *ex ante* modelling of the impacts of the tax and any rebates. These commissions can help to stimulate public debate of environmental and tax issues. Green tax commissions can accelerate the implementation of green tax reform by providing solutions to difficult issues and through improved perceptions of legitimacy. Different countries have examined different aspects of green tax reform, see Table 5.

The success of these green tax commissions has been mixed. The Swedish, Norwegian, Danish, and Dutch commissions generated proposals for green tax reform and facilitated the implementation of environmentally related taxes. The Japanese commission recommended the greater use of economic instruments, particularly environmentally related taxes.

The Danish experience with green tax commissions illustrates the operation of such a body. In 1993 the Danish government set up an inter-ministerial committee to analyse various possibilities for introducing green taxes and to develop models for phasing-in taxes and for recycling revenue. The committee also held meetings with industry, environmental, and consumer organisations. These stakeholders contributed to the reform process and suggested amendments to proposals. Similar procedures have been used in other countries.

Table 5. **Green Tax Commissions and their remit**

	Date of Introduction	Environmentally related taxes	Recycling revenues	Damaging subsidies	Other damaging effects of fiscal reform	Within the context of broader tax reform
Belgium	1993	Yes	Yes	No	No/n.a	n.a.
Denmark	1993	Yes	Yes	No	No	Yes
Finland	1991/1986	Yes	Yes	Yes/No	No	No
Ireland	1996/97	Yes	Yes	No	n.a.	n.a.
Italy	1996/97	Yes	Yes	No	n.a.	Yes
Japan	1994	Yes	Yes	Yes	No/n.a.	n.a.
Netherlands	1999/1995	Yes	Yes	No/n.a.	Yes	Yes
Norway	1994/1990	Yes	Yes	Yes	Yes	Yes
Sweden	1994	Yes	Yes	Yes	Yes	Yes

Notes: The official status of the commissions included in the table vary considerably, so does the approaches to any studies of possible uses of revenues raised (revenue recycling), and the follow-up of the proposals presented..
Source: Based on Schlegelmilch (1997).

A possible political benefit arising from a green tax commission is the creation of a social consensus for new or higher environmentally related taxes. Such a consensus is essential in order to reap the potential economic benefits of an environmentally related tax and recycling package. For example, if no consensus exists, then employees might claim wage compensation for higher energy prices above relief through direct taxes, which may lead to a wage-price spiral, which would negatively affect job creation. The green tax commission process may also improve the reception of new, and higher, environmentally related taxes by providing a forum to explain the objectives of the taxation, including the wider economic impacts of revenue recycling, *i.e.* the double environment employment dividend. The commissions may also attribute increased institutional and administrative capacity building and information exchange, to the commission, which in turn, facilitate the introduction of new taxes.

7.2. Other measures for acceptance building

A "greening" of the tax system can be undertaken in a comprehensive manner, with a role for a green tax commission, or more incrementally, with the case-by-case introduction of new or higher environmentally related taxation. In such situations other approaches to acceptance building are used, for example, careful planning of a new environmentally related tax, including simple and clear objectives, the diffusion of information, and time for consultation, including public hearings. A period of consultation enables various stakeholder groups to influence policy design and for the government to explain wider policy objectives. Early announcement of tax details, including tax rates, and gradual implementation of a new tax, gives taxpayers time to adapt their production, consumption and investment strategy to the new instrument. The earmarking of environmentally related taxation revenues is a widespread acceptance building measure, for example earmarking road taxation and fuel taxes to road building, returning taxes on industrial carbon emissions/energy use to industry via lower social security payments, and supporting environmental projects from waste taxation revenues.

7.2.1. *Other acceptance building measures in practice*

A recent example of acceptance building in the UK has been the three years of consultation on the appropriate policies to reduce industrial energy use. Consultation started with the Lord Marshall Report on "Economic Instruments and the Business Use of Energy" in 1998. The government's decision to follow the tax route, lead to two years of detailed consultation with industry, the trades unions,[2] and the public, on a "Climate Change Levy", and associated negotiated agreements, exemptions, support funds, etc. The tax was implemented in 2001 (see Box 14).

Box 14. **Acceptance building measures used for the UK tax on industry and business use of energy**

The following measures of acceptance building have been identified for the UK tax on industry and business use of energy (the "Climate Change Levy"):

- There was a clear environmental objective to which the government was publicly committed.
- The negotiation of the tax package was iterative.
- The package represents a balanced mix of economic instruments: environmental agreements, taxes and regulation.
- The tax includes an element of hypothecation to help the taxpayers reduce their energy consumption and therefore reduce their liability to tax; and
- The government has introduced compensatory tax cuts to employers' social security contributions.

Source: UK Roundtable (2000).

There are many examples of taxes with clear environmental objectives, for instance the US taxes on CFCs, Dutch taxation of chlorinated solvents, and environmental related taxation differentials for leaded-unleaded, high sulphur-low sulphur automotive fuels. Instances of early warning include the UK tax on the extraction of mineral aggregates, and the German energy tax reform package. These German taxes and the UK landfill tax are examples of progressive implementation – where government is committed to gradual and predictable tax rate rises.

The Dutch government has taken steps to promote confidence regarding tax relief in order to minimise the risks of claims for double compensation. One measure has been to ensure that tax and recycling bills are bound together by provisions that make the entry into force dependent on the entry to force of the other. Another measure is to introduce the tax in stages, and to incorporate temporary relief packages to reduce the immediate effect of the tax on the price index, thereby lowering the risk of claims for double compensation. The Danish government in implementing its energy tax package, made an agreement with industry, that it would undertake an *ex post* evaluation of the tax, to test its effectiveness and impact, and to adjust the tax as necessary. This assessment concluded that energy consumption in the industrial sector would have been 10% higher in 1997 if there had been no taxes on energy and furthermore that the system of energy efficiency agreements with energy-intensive sectors did reduce energy consumption. [Bjørner and Jensen (2000)].

Acceptance building measures are also important to maintain the consensus for implementing or increasing rates of environmentally related taxes regardless of exogenous impacts. For example, the UK Government chose to abandon the fuel duty escalator in favour of looking at the social, environmental and economic impact of fuel duty changes on a Budget by Budget basis. The importance of communicating the purpose of a new tax or tax rate increases to industry, trades unions, and the public, has been highlighted in the autumn 2000 European-wide protests at high oil prices and in particular high fuel duty. The Italian government responded to the recent increase in crude oil prices by postponing the implementation of its green tax reforms. The German government response to high crude oil prices was to introduce two new measures to offset increased energy costs to affected groups.[3] A single grant is provided to low-income households for the increased costs of heating. In addition, from 2001 all commuters, not only those commuting by car, will be able to claim income tax relief based on the distance travelled from home to work (the flat mileage rate will be increased and transformed to a distance mileage rate of 0.80 DM per kilometre).

NOTES

1. This section is in part based on Schlegelmilch (1997).
2. The UK government has also consulted with the trade unions, through the Trades Union Sustainable Development Advisory Committee. The remit of this committee is to provide Government with a Trade Union perspective on the employment consequences of climate change, and the response to it and to allow the Trades Unions to enter into constructive dialogue with the Government on sustainable development and environmental issues'.
3. For additional information concerning acceptance-building in Germany, see Schlegelmilch (2000).

Chapter 8

ENVIRONMENTAL EFFECTIVENESS: AVAILABLE EVIDENCE

The environmental effectiveness of a tax can be measured as the extent to which the tax delivers a reduction in pollution or actual emissions. The quantitative emissions reduction effect of a tax depends on the response of the polluter to the price incentive. The own-price elasticities estimated for energy sources are generally fairly low, albeit significantly different from zero. Increasing tax rates on relatively inelastically demanded goods will reduce consumption, however the environmental impact will in general be fairly modest in the short-term, whilst tax revenues will increase. In the long-term energy price elasticities are generally larger and therefore the environmental effectiveness of the tax will increase. Evaluations of the environmental effectiveness of environmentally related taxation are not routinely carried out, perhaps in part because it is often difficult to isolate the impact of the tax alone from other elements of a policy package on consumption/production. A lack of data on emissions and the means to measure the longer-term impacts of taxes on technological change also complicates the measuring of environmental effectiveness.

8.1. Price elasticities: behavioural responses[1]

It is possible to measure the magnitude of the demand change resulting from higher prices following changes in taxation. These estimates can help policymakers predict the environmental effectiveness and the revenues raised by an environmentally related tax. An important first step in evaluating behavioural responses to environmentally related taxes is the collection of, and regular updating of, information on the price elasticities of demand for energy, transport and other environmentally related goods. Box 15 explains the elasticity terms used in this section.

Behavioural responses to environmental taxes can be estimated *ex ante* (predicted values) or evaluated *ex post* (actual values). The *ex ante* approach uses econometric methods to estimate price elasticities, which, with precaution, are used to predict behavioural responses to environmental taxes. The main advantage of the price elasticity estimates approach is that it does not require that a tax be implemented, merely that relative prices change. This is important in view of the fact that many environmentally related taxes have only a short history. Although general price elasticity estimates have been derived for many countries and for several years, empirical data on consumer responses to environmentally related taxes are scarce [Ekins and Speck (1998*b*) and OECD (1997)].

Ex *post* estimates concentrate on the absolute reduction in consumption (final or intermediate) caused by the introduction or increase of an environmental tax in a specific country at a specific time [see EEA (1996) and Ekins and Speck (1998*b*)]. Such studies are relevant for future modifications and adjustments of the environmental tax in the country concerned. In addition, *ex post* studies may provide useful information as input for tax impact studies focusing on other countries. However very few *ex post* studies have been undertaken.

As experience in environmentally related taxes grows, an increasing body, albeit still limited, of estimates has become available. Most of the taxes apply to the energy and transport sectors and therefore it is not surprising that most demand price elasticities focus on energy and transport. There are also a few demand elasticity estimates for non-energy and non-transport environmental goods. A few estimates are presented below.

Box 15.   The main elasticity terms

(Own-)*Price elasticity*: is a measure of the responsiveness of demand (supply) to a change in price, defined as the percentage change of demand (supply) per percentage change of the price. The own-price elasticity of demand reflects current preferences (consumer demand), technology (producer demand of intermediate goods), and availability of substitute goods. Since all these basic characteristics can change, especially in the long run, the changes in prices have normally a larger impact in the *long run* than in the short run, *i.e.* the long term elasticity is higher than the short term one.

Inelastic demand is when the price elasticity is, in absolute terms, smaller than 1. This means that an x% increase of prices would lead to a less than x% reduction of demand. However behavioural impacts could still be significant.

Cross-price demand elasticity is a measure of the responsiveness of demand of one good to a change in price of another good. For example, the impact on demand for natural gas following an increase in the price of electricity will be higher than following a price increase for aviation fuel, as natural gas and electricity are in some situations substitute fuels, whereas natural gas and aviation fuel are not.

Source: Based on OECD (2000*a*).

8.1.1. *Energy demand price elasticities*

There are demand own-price elasticities for each type of energy and fuel. Cross-price elasticities between substitute fuels are also important in determining the fuel or fuel mix chosen. Estimates show that, in most cases, demand for total energy use is rather inelastic in the short term; estimates for short run own-price elasticities range between –0.13 to –0.26. However, long run elasticities are significantly higher (–0.37 to –0.46). This would mean that the impact of an energy tax would be larger in the longer term.

Studies on the price elasticities for gasoline show comparable, albeit less homogeneous results. While most estimates show low own-price elasticities in the short run (–0.15 to –0.28), some estimates indicate significantly higher values (–0.51 to –1.07). Long-term own-price elasticities are estimated to be higher (0.23 to –1.05). There are differences between countries and variances are mainly explained by the use of different estimation methods. This uncertainty could be reduced through comparisons of *ex ante* and *ex post* estimates.

In the last decade, market liberalisation and increased competition in the energy markets has contributed to lower energy prices and increased energy demand in many OECD Member countries. The trend is for further liberalisation of energy markets with expected price cuts in OECD countries in the coming years. It is against this background of falling prices (market signals working in the opposite direction) that environmentally related taxes may be introduced or modified. However, crude oil price increases during 2000 mean that prices facing energy users have increased since these elasticity estimates were calculated. Studies of behavioural impacts of the recent increases in crude oil prices would be most useful. Although energy demand is relatively inelastic, a price elasticity significantly different from zero indicates that price increases can substantially reduce the demand for energy. Environmentally related taxes could have a significant impact on reducing energy demand, especially in the long run.

8.1.2. *Energy cross-price elasticities*

Cross-price elasticities measure the impact of a change of price of one product, for example petrol, on the demand for substitute products, for example diesel and LPG. Changes in relative tax rates

Table 6.   **Selected estimates of price elasticity of gasoline**

		Short run	Long run	Ambiguous
Pooled time-series/ cross-section	Micro	−0.30 to −0.39 (USA)	−0.77 to −0.83 (USA)	
	Macro	−0.15 to −0.38 (OECD[1]) −0.15 (Europe) −0.6 (Mexico)	−1.05 to −1.4 (OECD[1]) −1.24 (Europe) −0.55 to −0.9 (OECD 18[2]) −1.25 to −1.13 (Mexico)	
Cross-section	Micro	−0.51 (USA) 0 to −0.67 (USA)		
	Macro	Mean −1.07 (−0.77 to −1.34)(OECD[1])		
Time-series	Micro			
	Macro	−0.12 to −0.17 (USA)	−0.23 to −0.35 (USA)	
Meta-analyses and surveys		Avg. −0.26 (0 to −1.36) (International) Mean −0.27 (Time-series) Mean −0.28 (Cross-sect.) −0.26	Avg. −0.58 (0 to −2.72) (International) Mean −0.71 (Time-series) Mean −0.84 (Cross-sect.) Mean −0.86	Avg. −0.53 (−0.02 to −1.59) (USA) Mean −0.53 (Time-series) Mean −0.18 (Cross-section) −0.53 (Panel data) −0.1 to −0.3 (22 estimates)

1. OECD except Luxembourg, Iceland, and New Zealand.
2. OECD 18 countries include: Canada, US, Japan, Austria, Belgium, Denmark, France, Germany, Greece, Ireland, Italy, Netherlands, Norway, Spain, Sweden, Switzerland, Turkey, and UK.
Source: OECD (2000*a*).

Table 7.   **Selected estimates of own-price elasticity of residential electricity**

		Short run	Long run	Ambiguous
Pooled time-series/ cross-section	Micro	−0.433 (Norway) −0.2 (US)	−0.442 (Norway)	
	Macro	−0.158 to −0.184 (USA)	−0.263 to −0.329 (USA)	
Cross-section	Micro	0.4 to −1.1 (Norway)	0.3 to −1.1 (Norway)	
	Macro			−1.42 (53 countries)
Time-series	Macro	−0.25 (USA) −0.62 (USA)	−0.5 (USA) −0.6 (USA)	
Meta-analyses and surveys		−0.05 to −0.9	−0.2 to −4.6	−0.05 to −0.12 (4 studies)

Source: OECD (2000*a*).

between different substitute fuels could be used to encourage fuel-switching to lower-carbon energy sources for electricity generation and to less polluting automotive fuels. The impact of such differentials on structural change in the energy and fuel markets is likely to be larger in the long run, when elasticities are, in general, larger. In most OECD countries, the tax differentiation between *leaded and unleaded petrol*, combined with a series of other measures,[2] led to a rapid fall in consumption and in the share of leaded petrol, which is now withdrawn from sale in many OECD countries. The fiscal incentive greatly speeded up the process.

Governments should take into account the impact of cross price elasticities when designing new taxes, to avoid negative environmental impacts. For example, the UK government has offered a five year special rebate in Northern Ireland only for natural gas from the forthcoming tax on energy use in business and industry. The Northern Ireland gas market is not well developed. Therefore it was feared that any price increases for gas following the implementation of the new tax would reinforce the widespread use of substitute fuels, in particular heavy oil and coal.

8.1.3. Transport price elasticities

There are fewer studies on the demand price elasticity of non-energy products. However, an exception is estimates of transport demand own-price elasticities. Table 8 shows that the demand for private motoring is relatively inelastic, though in the longer-run higher motoring costs would lead to significant reductions in automobile transport. Demand elasticities for urban transit are rather low (in absolute terms) in the short run, perhaps the result of limited viable alternatives. However, in the longer term, demand is estimated to be more elastic. Long-term price elasticity for the number of kilometres driven has been estimated between –0.1 and-0.4 [Van Wee (1995) and Kleijn and Klooster (1990)]. The price elasticity for car ownership is estimated to be –0.1 [European Commission (1997)]. Demand price elasticities for air and inter-city rail transport are estimated to be higher than for automobile and urban transit modes.

Table 8. **Elasticity for modes of transport**

	Short run	Long run	Ambiguous
Elasticity for automobile	–0.09 to –0.24	–0.22 to –0.31	–0.13 to –0.52
Elasticity for urban transit			
Time-Series			–0.01 to –1.32*
Cross-section			–0.05 to –0.34
Pooled data			–0.06 to –0.44
	Time-series		Cross-section
Elasticity for air travel			
Leisure	–0.4 to –1.98		–1.52
Business	–0.65		–1.15
Mixed or unknown	–0.36 to –1.81		–0.76 to –4.51
Elasticity for inter-city rail			
Leisure	–0.67 to –1.00		–0.7
Mixed or unknown	–0.37 to –1.5		–1.4

* Most values fall between –0.1 an –0.6.
Source: OECD (2000a).

8.1.4. Other price elasticities

There are fewer demand price elasticity estimates for non-energy and non-transport related goods. Estimates for the price elasticity of demand for pesticides range from –0.2 to –0.5 [EIM (1999)] but price elasticity of demand for herbicides, fungicides and insecticides is higher. Data from the price effects of the Swedish tax on fertilisers suggest that the own-price elasticity of demand of chemical nitrogen fertiliser in Sweden is between 0.17 and –0.25.

Initial estimates of groundwater consumption elasticities in the Netherlands range between –0.05 and –0.30.[3] EPA (2001) concludes in a section on water fees in United States that "Although water demand is often assumed to be inelastic, studies that separate water demand by season have found that household water demand is inelastic in winter but elastic in summer. Others have found that water demand by industrial and agricultural users is sensitive to price changes."

8.1.5. Supply elasticities

Environmentally related taxation will also affect supply, possibly through domestic firms producing less or moving abroad. However, there is little conclusive empirical evidence that environmentally related taxes lead firms to set up in countries with lower taxation. This is not surprising, since most environmentally related taxes have been introduced with numerous associated exemptions and rebates, precisely to avoid such locational displacement. It may be that in the future higher environmentally related taxation will cause production to shift, in those sectors where capital is sufficiently mobile, to countries were taxes are lower. However, it is also possible that some of the current exemptions are "unnecessary", because competitiveness impacts are more apparent than real. Those who benefit from existing exemptions obviously have a strong incentive to argue in favour of their continuation.

8.1.6. Future efforts

Future research should examine closer the linkage between environmentally related taxes and relative price effects, *i.e.* the incidence of the tax.

Predicting behavioural responses on the basis of estimated price elasticities has its limitations. Nevertheless, the available data on own-price elasticities shows that although the demand for automotive fuels, domestic electricity, and transportation modes is relatively inelastic, in most cases the elasticities are still significantly different from zero. Therefore, environmentally related taxes, by raising the prices of such products, can result in significant reductions in demand and pollution. This reduction would be expected to be, in the majority of the cases, larger in the long than in the short run. In the long run, economic agents have a wider range of options available for responding, such as new techniques, reorganisation, shifts to other goods and services, investment, relocation, etc.

More could be done to improve long-run elasticity estimates to capture the full impact of taxation on investment, production and consumption decisions. Experiments (using simulated, but complete, systems of demand functions) and comparing *ex ante* with *ex post* estimates would be useful in improving elasticity estimates. The oil price increases experienced during 2000 could prove a good case study to further understanding of energy price elasticities. Furthermore, elasticities could be used to test the effectiveness of complementary policy instruments, for example energy efficiency information and advice for households and industry aimed at reducing energy demand. Evidence of the environmental effectiveness of environmentally related taxes in use confirms that taxation can be an effective policy option to bring about reductions in polluting activity. Nevertheless, most countries do apply numerous rebates and exemptions that reduce the environmental effectiveness of the taxes.

8.2. Empirical evidence for environmental effectiveness of taxes

8.2.1. Fuel taxes

Table 6 shows that demand price elasticities for gasoline are rather low, but nevertheless significantly different from zero, even in the short run. Over a longer period, fuel taxes and fuel prices can have considerable impact on the use of vehicles, *i.e.* kilometres driven, and on the choice between different types of vehicle. An illustration in given in Figure 13.

The figure shows the fuel efficiency of new vehicles sold in United States and the end-user price of petrol, adjusted for inflation over the period 1970-1997. While more detailed studies would be needed to determine the precise interaction, at this level of aggregation the fuel efficiency of new cars, measured in kilometres per litre, and the petrol price develop together. After initial rises in the 1970s, the levelling off of the petrol price below the level in 1970 goes hand in hand with a stagnation in the increase of fuel efficiency of new cars.

In the UK, the road fuel duty escalator, abandoned in 2000, raised real fuel prices by 6% per annum. An evaluation calculated that – if the escalator had been kept in place over the period 1996 to 2002 (the originally planned lifetime of the escalator) – the escalator would reduce annual carbon dioxide emissions by between 2 and 5 million tonnes of carbon by 2010, *i.e.* a reduction of between 4.6% and 11.5%.[4] The conclusion of another report was that the escalator had dynamic efficiency benefits by creating incentives for on-going fuel economy: average fuel efficiency of articulated lorries more than 33 tonnes increased by 13% between 1993 and 1998 [DETR (1999)].

Figure 13. **Petrol prices and fuel efficiency of new cars**
United States

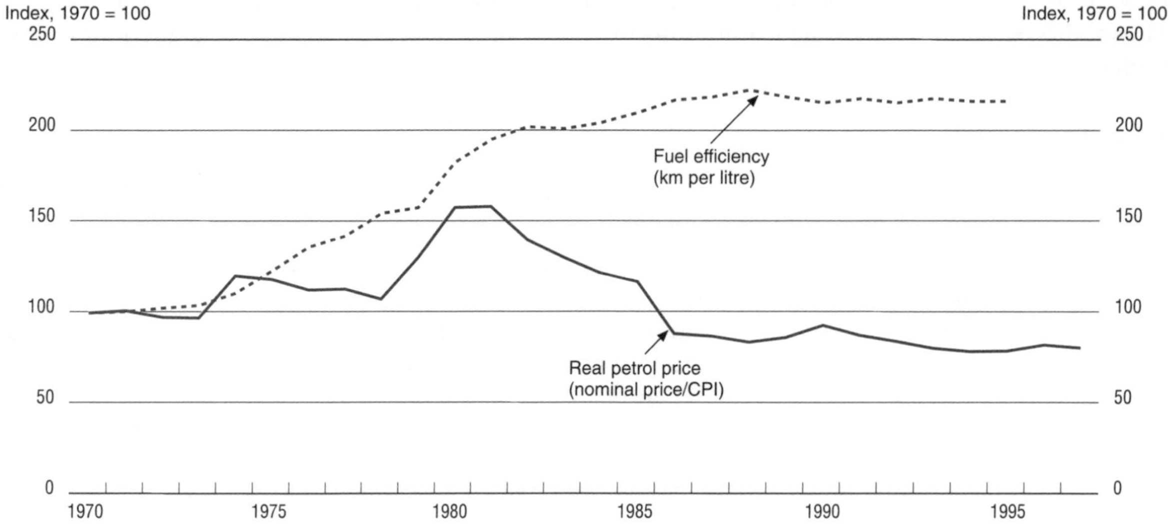

Index, 1970 = 100

Fuel efficiency
(km per litre)

Real petrol price
(nominal price/CPI)

Index, 1970 = 100

Source: Birol and Keppler (2000).

8.2.2. Vehicle taxes

Vehicle purchase and registration taxes account for half of all the tax bases in the OECD/EU database on environmentally related taxes. These taxes may provide incentives for lower car ownership and/or less use. One-off sales or registration taxes can impact on the decision whether or not to buy a vehicle, and on the types of vehicles bought, depending on the structure of the tax rates. However, once the vehicle is bought, such taxes do not influence directly how much the vehicle is used. Annual taxes on motor vehicle usage can also impact on the decision on what type of vehicle is bought, and on whether or not to maintain the permission to use the vehicle the coming period. They can also be formulated in ways that influence usage more directly, like the taxes on diesel vehicles in New Zealand that are levied per 1 000 km driven. Deposit-refund systems and various types of scrapping schemes can – to some extent – influence the age composition of the vehicle stock.

Car ownership is relatively price inelastic, and therefore fairly high taxes would be required to have a significant impact [Van Wee (1995) see also Section 8.1.3]. There is, however, some evidence that the very high car registration fees applied in Denmark and Norway has resulted in the vehicle stock generally to be relatively old compared to the situation in other countries. In isolation, this could be negative from an environmental point of view. The registration fees do, however, also contribute to the vehicles being relatively small and fuel-efficient.

German vehicle circulation tax rates are determined by emission rates; passenger cars classified as low-pollutant or low-fuel consumption are subject to reduced tax rates. There is evidence that these differential tax rates have been environmental effective. From July 1997 to January 2000 the stock of high-emission cars was reduced from 6.9 million to 3 million cars. In the same period the stock of vehicles that fulfil the EURO 2, 3, and 4 standards increased from 6.2 million to nearly 16 million cars (total car stock 42.4 million) [see Jatzke (2000)].

In 1993 Sweden introduced differentiated registration taxes based on environmental criteria. Taxes were raised for class 3 cars and lowered for "cleaner" class 1 cars. The share of class 1 and class 2 cars in newly registered vehicles rose from 16 to 75% in the period 1993 to 1996. The Swedish EPA (1997) attributes this change in purchasing patterns more to "soft effects" resulting from advertising and consumer awareness than to the tax itself, because the tax had a small impact on the purchase price of a car.

The Austrian vehicle taxation influences the fuel consumption of the vehicles in several ways: The rate of the car registration tax is directly dependent on the (EU-)norm fuel consumption, and the annual vehicle tax is dependent on the engine power of a car, which is highly correlated to fuel consumption. A number of other OECD countries, for example Denmark, Norway and Germany do differentiate annual auto taxes on the basis of environmental criteria.

There are no studies that calculate the impact of annual motor vehicle taxes. The European Commission (1997) cautions that the environmental effectiveness of such taxes is likely to be low. First, because cars that are more fuel efficient, and therefore have lower variable costs, might encourage more kilometres to be driven. Second, the price elasticity of both vehicle ownership and the number of kilometres driven is low, and therefore, small tax differentials are unlikely to have significant direct effects. The second argument used here does, however, seem to limit the importance of the first argument raised.

8.2.3. "Carbon" and energy taxes

CO_2-related taxes have been implemented in Denmark, Finland, Italy, Norway, the Netherlands and Sweden. There are few *ex post* evaluations of these taxation. All the countries apply a large number of exemptions and rebates to these taxes which in practice means that a significant proportion of total carbon emissions are untaxed, thereby reducing the environmental effectiveness of the taxes. It is also important to include other energy taxes (and any changes made in these) when studying the impacts of CO_2-related taxes. It is the total tax rate on each carbon-containing fuel (and the tax rates on any non-carbon energy sources) that together will influence the impact on CO_2 emissions.

One of the few *ex post* evaluations available was undertaken in 1995 for the Swedish Environment Protection Agency (Naturvårdsverket, 1995). The study showed that CO_2-emissions from the district heating, industrial and housing sectors were about 8 million tons (19%) lower in 1994 than in 1987. The study estimated that 60% of the emission reduction was caused by the CO_2 taxation. Over the same period, emissions from the transport sector increased 5.5 million tons. The estimated emission reduction in the district heating, industrial and housing sectors can seem rather large, given the short time period the CO_2 tax had been in place, and the limited tax changes a number of large emitters were facing.

Larsen and Nesbakken (1996) calculated that the Norwegian CO_2 tax introduced in 1991, reduced CO_2 emissions at stationary combustion plants by 21% by 1995. In other sectors, the emissions reduction was less, for example emissions produced by mobile household combustion devices fell by between 2% and 3% as a consequence of the CO_2 tax. ECON (1994) calculated that CO_2 emissions per unit of oil produced by the Norwegian oil sector fell by 1.5% due to measures taken by the industry in response to the CO_2 tax.[5]

In 1999 a working group to the Finish Economic Council undertook an evaluation of the effectiveness of Finish energy and carbon taxation [Finish Economic Council (2000)]. The report estimates what CO_2 emissions would have been in the absence of increased taxation, and concludes that carbon emissions would have been 4 million tonnes, or 7%, higher in 1998, if taxes had remained at the 1990 level. The report estimates that reduced petrol consumption, and structural and consumption changes in industry both resulted in reduction of carbon emissions by 1 million tonnes in the period. Two thirds of the reduction in industrial carbon emissions resulted from fuel switching away from coal and heavy fuel oil towards natural gas. Changes in the fuel mix for electricity and heat production accounted for the remaining 2 million tonnes reduction in carbon emissions.

Ex *ante* estimates of environmental effectiveness are also undertaken in many countries. The Danish energy policy package introduced in 1995 is expected to reduce CO_2 emissions by 3.8% by 2005, of which 2% attributable to taxes [Danish Government (1999a)].The UK government has estimated that its tax on industry and business use of energy would reduce carbon-equivalent emissions by just

2 million tonnes in 2010 or by just over 1% of total emissions. The entire package with tax, negotiated agreements (2.5 MtC), and energy efficiency support (0.5 MtC) is expected to reduce carbon equivalent emissions by 5 million tonnes of carbon by 2010.

The intense debate following the proposals for new energy taxation in Germany, introduced in 1999, produced some analysis of the effectiveness of both the electricity tax and the increases in mineral oil taxation. Of particular interest is an assessment of the impact of tax exemptions and rebates on the environmental effectiveness of the taxes (see Table 9). By 2003 the reform will redistribute 2%-3% of the total German tax revenue. Assuming price elasticities for fuel demand in the order of 0.2 to 0.3, the potential reductions in demand, resulting from the fuel tax increases, are likely to be in the order of 3%-5%, compared to a business as usual scenario. The tax-induced reduction in CO_2 emissions is estimated to be in the order of 9 million tonnes, less than 2% of total emissions (half of this reduction is expected from reductions in passenger car kilometres) [RWI (1999)].

The result of these rebates and exemptions is that different energy sources are taxed in an unequal manner without justification in terms of carbon emissions. This undermines both the environmental and economic efficiency of the taxes. For example, energy generated from oil and gas is effectively taxed twice: by the mineral oil tax and the electricity tax. Nuclear and coal generated electricity (and renewable energy), in turn, is taxed only once by the electricity tax. If the environmental impact of different energy sources is measured in terms of CO_2 emissions, the marginal tax burden of the additional taxes for the release of an additional tonne of CO_2 varied between nil and DM36/tonne of CO_2 in the first year of the reform (1999). In 2003, the range will be greater from nil to DM116/tonne of CO_2 (Table 9). The total tax burden, *i.e.* including the burden of all other taxation on energy, is shown in the final column of the table. The German *energy* taxes by exempting highly efficient gas-fired CCGTs and efficient co-generation from the mineral oil tax creates some incentives to move away from coal to gas, however, coal, the most CO_2 intensive fuel, remains untaxed.

Table 9. **The German ecological tax reform – differences in the additional tax burden between fuels**

	Taxation before reform	Increases in 1999	Ecotax burden of 1999 tax increases (DM per ton of CO_2 emission)	Total tax burden, *i.e;* the sum of all taxation energy in 2003 (DM per ton of CO_2 emision)
Coal	–	–	0	0
Gas (Pf/kWh)	0.36	0.32	16	34
Fuel oil (Pk/1)	8	4	13	46
Electricity (Pf/kWh)	–	2	36	71
Diesel (Pf/1)	62	6	21	347
Petrol (Pf/1)	98	6	24	549

Source: Umwelt-Gutachten (2000).

8.2.4. SO_2 and NO_x taxation

Ex *post* analysis of the Swedish sulphur tax (introduced in 1991) shows that the tax contributed to emissions of sulphur dioxide declining by 80% compared to 1980 levels [Nordic Council of Ministers (1999)]. Taxes on sulphur is estimated to have contributed 30% of the total reduction in sulphur emissions from 1989 to 1995, *i.e.* 19 000 tonnes of SO_2, or 20% of total emissions in 1995 [Swedish EPA (1997)]. The tax has been effective at reducing the sulphur content of light oils which has now fallen below 0.076% (*i.e.* less than half the legal limit of 0.2%).

Danish SO_2 emissions were reduced by 24% in the period 1995-1997 [Danish Government (1999a)]. Within a few weeks of the implementation of the tax, the sulphur content of fuel gas oil and heavy fuel reduced from 0.2% to 0.05% and by a third for coal. This response confirmed a Ministry of Taxation survey that found there were no price differentials between high and low sulphur fuels, prior to the tax, and therefore, the tax generated incentives for a rapid shift to low sulphur fuels and coal. The tax has had some dynamic efficiency effects through forcing the development of sulphur purification plants and technology [Danish Ministry of Taxation (1998)]. Larsen (2000) also indicate that the tax has been more effective than foreseen when it was implemented. In 1995 it was estimated that the tax would raise 715 million DKK in revenues in 2000, while the revenue estimate is now revised downwards to 275 million DKK.

The Swedish NO_x charge on measured emissions from large combustion plants has contributed to lower emissions at the regulated plants. Revenues from the charge are fully refunded to polluters in proportion to their share of net energy output, thereby creating additional incentives for energy efficiency in energy generation. Average NO_x emissions (not only in those plants that are taxed), have fallen from 0.41 kg per MWh of energy generated in 1992, the year the tax was introduced, to 0.26 kg per MWh in 1996. However, this figure is an average for all plants, including those not subject to the charge, and many plants are also subject to local regulations. The Swedish EPA estimates that without the charge NO_x emissions would have been 25% higher from combustion in 1995. However, the charge has also resulted in *higher* emissions of other pollutants, namely N_2O (Swedish EPA, 1997).

8.2.5. *Taxation of Ozone Depleting Chemicals* (ODC)

A number of countries (Czech Republic, Hungary, Poland, Sweden, and the US) apply environmentally related taxes to ODCs. In the US ODCs are both taxed and traded. The tax in itself will not impact on sales, if all the tradable quotas are taken up. In theory, the taxes will reduce the price of the quota, but the sum of the quota price and tax will stay the same: determined by the demand and (vertical) supply curves for quotas. At the same time, the sales of ODCs will remain equal to the total quota volume. However, the different tax rates applied to different ODCs may have created incentives for the acceleration of the market exit of some products and the development of substitute products for domestic and export markets [Cook (1996)].

EPA (2001) states that "the tax" on ozone-depleting chemicals "is believed to have contributed significantly to the reduction in ODC use. Several other factors, however, also had an impact, including the establishment of an ODC trading system. … As a result of the multiplicity of these policy measures, it is difficult to isolate the effects of the CFC tax".

8.2.6. *Waste taxes*

Waste taxes have the potential not only to create incentives for waste minimisation and to encourage reuse and recycling, but also for relatively cheap greenhouse gas, specifically methane, emissions reduction.

The Danish non-hazardous waste tax has reduced net delivered waste to municipal sites by 26% in the period 1987-1996, and waste to smaller fills and private waste sites, by 39% in the period 1990-1996.[6] The breakdown in waste reduction varied between different waste streams; building and construction industry was cut by 63%, household waste by 16%, whilst trade and industry waste increased by 8% in the 1987-1996 period. The tax has been decisive in reducing taxable waste, particularly construction and demolition waste. The authors note that other measures introduced at the same time as the waste tax, could also account for a proportion of the waste reduction. In another evaluation Andersen (1998) found that the tax created incentives for recycling which increased considerably in the period: by 77% for paper and cardboard, and by 50% for glass.

Ex *post* analysis of the UK landfill tax shows that the tax has had a mixed impact depending on waste stream: household, municipal, commercial and industrial, and construction and demolition waste.[7] HM Customs and Excise data show that "standard' rate waste fell only marginally between 1997/98 and 1998/99, waste under the "reduced' rate declined by 15% and "exempt' waste deposited at landfills reduced by 8.5% in the period. However, the data indicate that municipal waste has increased by around 3% per annum, since the introduction of the tax. The tax has had no impact on this waste stream because households are not directly subject to the tax, and therefore they have no incentives for waste minimisation. The tax has created incentives for some local authorities to increase composting facilities and kerbside recycling. Of 26 million tonnes of domestic waste in England and Wales in 1995/96 only 4.7% was composted or recycled. This increased to 8.5% of total domestic waste in 1999. There is also some evidence that the tax (backed by the government's Environmental Technology Best Practice programme) has been effective at reducing commercial and industrial waste and boosting recycling rates. Construction and demolition waste deposited in landfills has fallen from 42 million tonnes pre tax to 24 million tonnes post tax. There is some evidence of increased dumping of inert waste at unlicensed sites, for example on farms and golf courses, for spurious land reclamation purposes. The government has responded to this problem by offering an exemption for waste used legitimately to restore landfills and by appropriate regulatory action.

In the United States, more than 4 200 local communities in 42 States apply charges on household waste, which are calculated according to the volumes discharged. The taxes resulted in a significant reduction in the volume of discarded waste and a significant increase in recycling [Anderson *et al.* (1997), EPA (2001)]. As mentioned in Section 6.2, EPA (2001) quotes studies that indicate that introduction of a weight-based waste collection system in Seattle caused the weight of collected garbage to decrease 15%.

Austrian waste disposal charges are differentiated by the efficiency of the facility. The charges have created incentives for the improvement in landfill management. In 1996/97 21 landfill facilities in Austria did not meet "state-of-the-art' standards, by 1999 only four sites failed the efficiency test [Unweltbundesamt (2000)].

8.2.7. *Packaging taxes*

In 1998 Denmark altered their packaging tax from a pure volume based tax, to one with some weight-based elements. The intention was to generate incentives for producers to reduce the amount of materials used for packaging [Danish EPA (2000)]. There are also proposals to improve the environmental linkage of these taxes to the environmental damage caused by different packaging materials, *i.e.* lower taxes would apply to paper and glass, and higher tax rates to aluminium and polyvinyl chloride.

8.2.8. *Other non-energy product taxes*

The Danish tax on nickel-cadmium (NiCd) batteries introduced in 1996 has resulted in increased collection rates and changes to the household electronic market. Battery collection increased from 30 tonnes per year to 100 tonnes in 1997. The tax rebate for battery collection is determined by weight, this has created additional incentives for heavier professional use batteries to be returned. There is some evidence that the tax has reduced the use of batteries [Danish Government (1999a)]. The Swedes also introduced a charge on batteries in 1996 with rates in 2001 depending on the type of battery (alkaline/mercury oxide/zinc-air batteries 500 SEK per kg, nickel-cadmium 300 SEK per kg and lead starter batteries 30 SEK per each, and other lead batteries 1.70 SEK per kg). The Swedish EPA (1997) conclude that the tax has not affected purchasing patterns, but tax rates have since been increased substantially. The revenues from the tax have been used to finance the disposal of used batteries, and increased the collection and recycling rates for batteries: 100% of lead batteries, 60-70% of mercury and 35% of NiCd batteries were collected.

The Danish tax on chlorinated solvents introduced in 1996 has lead to a marked reduction in the consumption of trichloroethene (TRI) and tetrachloroethene (PER) and accelerated the complete removal of dichloromethane from market in 1998. The reduction in PER consumption was less than anticipated, which is the result of unforeseen substitution barriers. Revenues from the taxes declined from 3.3 million DKK in 1996 to 2.5 million DKK in 1998 as the tax base (pollution) contracted.

The Danish parliament introduced a tax on pesticides in 1995, and increased the tax rates in 1998, in order to meet the objectives of the domestic pesticide action plan. The average tax is 35% of retail sale value (exc. taxes). An *ex ante* assessment of the tax estimated that pesticide consumption would be reduced by between 5% and 10% based on a -0.5 price elasticity. In practice consumption of different pesticides declined by between 10% to 13% from 1995/96 to 1997, however it is not clear that this decline is attributable to the tax [Danish Government (1999b)]. A doubling of tax rate in 1998 is expected to reduce consumption by a further 8% to 10%.

Sweden implemented a pesticides tax in 1984 at a rate of 4 SEK (0.44€) per active kilo substance the rate was raised in 1994 to 20 SEK (2.2 €).[8] The tax is levied on pesticide manufacturers and importers. Evaluation of the impact of the tax on pesticide use has been complicated by other policy changes, for example the ban of certain pesticide products and also changes in the climate. However, the Swedish EPA calculated that the tax rate (8% of the purchase price) was too low to impact on user behaviour. In Sweden the main effects of the pesticide tax were attributed to "soft" effects, *i.e.* financing research and training and best practice [see Swedish EPA (1997) and Section 2.5.1]. Taxation of fertilisers in Sweden has been estimated to have reduced total nitrogen dosage by about 10% and the phosphate content by an unknown quantity [Swedish EPA (1997)].

Denmark implemented a tax on carrier bags made of plastic and paper in 1994. An *ex ante* evaluation estimated that revenue from the tax would be DKK275 million in 1994 (compared to a business as usual DKK500 million), however, the actual revenue raised from the tax was lower because the reduction in consumption was larger than expected, *i.e.* the tax has been more environmentally effective. After two years the revenue stabilised at around DKK140 million to DKK150 million, and achieved a 50% cut in the consumption of plastic bags.

8.2.9. *Water and wastewater taxes*

The Netherlands implemented a tax on groundwater in 1995. Water companies, agriculture, and industry subject to the tax to the extraction of groundwater (see Box 13 for the tax rates). A number of exemptions apply, for example water for irrigating agricultural land if less than 40 000 m^3 per year is extracted, emergency abstractions and extractions for ice skating rinks. Vermeend and van der Vaart (1998) evaluated the environmental effectiveness of the tax. The tax has doubled the price of self-abstracted water for agriculture and industries. Water companies have passed through the tax onto higher prices for the end-users they supply, *i.e.* households (+27%) and industry (+40%). Initial estimates of groundwater consumption elasticities were in the range −0.05 to −0.30. Using 1997 data groundwater consumption had reduced by between 2% and 12%. Their assessment also concluded that tax-exempt, small-scale groundwater extraction by households and agriculture, had increased. The Green Tax Commission has recommended an end to the partial exemptions offered for the self-abstraction of groundwater. Removal of the exemption is expected to result in the substitution of groundwater abstractions by increasing use of low-quality water by industry.[9]

Denmark also levies a water supply tax. It was implemented in 1993 with phased-in tax rate increases. The rate in 1998 was 5 DKK (0.68 €) per m^3 of piped water. The tax is levied on metered water, but if metered water amounts to less than 90% of water abstracted by the water company, including private water works, then the water company is liable to pay the tax. This tax rule creates incentives for water companies to reduce leakage rates. The environmental effectiveness of the tax is a little complicated to calculate because sewerage costs have also increased significantly over the same period. The average water bill has risen from 12 DKK per m^3 in 1989 to an estimated 25 DKK per m^3 in 2000, with half of the increase attributable to the water supply tax. Household water consumption has fallen by 26% in the period 1989 to 1998, with a 13% decline since the introduction of the tax in 1993. A survey carried out be Statistics Denmark in 1999, indicates that almost half of Danish households have responded to water price increases by investing in water saving appliances. Institutional and business water consumption contracted by 15% in the period. Furthermore, the tax has contributed to better water management by the water companies: in the period 1993-1998 leakage rates were reduced by 23%.

Germany has implemented wastewater taxation since 1981. The tax rate has increased progressively from 12 DM (6.12 €) to 70 DM (35.70 €) per damage unit in 1997. A damage unit varies by pollutant, for example 50kg of chemical oxygen demand, and 500 grams of lead, are both a damage unit. The tax is levied on direct discharges from industries and municipal sewage outlets. Rebates are offered if (best available technology, BAT) standards for sewage discharges are met, and further reduced, if water quality exceeds the standards and the discharge is part of a performance program. Exemptions for a number of industry sectors, for example pulp and paper, were offered up until 1989. The environmental effectiveness of the tax is hard to discern from the BAT standards, however, polluters have had an additional incentive to reduce discharges liable to the tax. Industrial discharges declined by 31% between 1981 and 1995 [Statistisches Bundesamt (1998)]. The impact of the tax on consumers is difficult to quantify. The wastewater tax forms a small proportion of overall municipal user fees for wastewater and the tax is not specified in these fees. Revenues from the tax are earmarked for improvements in municipal sewage treatment. Similar arguments are made concerning the impact of the Danish wastewater tax on households [Ecotec (2000)].

Water use in Brisbane, Australia, has been reduced by 20% between 1995-96 and 1997-98, after the adoption of metering and use-based charges.

8.2.10. *Mineral aggregates taxes*

The Danish tax on raw materials is levied on a number of raw materials, for example gravel and limestone, either extracted in Denmark, or imported. The tax is levied at a rate of 5 DKK per m^3 of raw material extracted. A number of exemptions apply, for example for raw materials extracted for coastal protection and recycled materials. The environmental effectiveness of the extraction tax, in terms of reducing extraction from quarries, is difficult to disentangle from the impact of the waste tax and from the economic (construction) cycle. However, the mineral aggregates and waste taxes together have impacted on the market for recycled materials; 90% of all demolition waste is now recycled.

8.3. Empirical evidence for the environmental effectiveness of tax differentials

8.3.1. *Energy tax rate differentials*

A number of tax rate differentials based on the relative environmental impact of substitute products and activities have had significant impacts on behaviour. Examples include the differentiation in tax rates between leaded and unleaded petrol, and between oils with different sulphur contents. In a similar way, it is believed that low relative tax rates on diesel compared to those levied on petrol, has influenced the composition of the car fleet. These examples are of near-perfect substitutes between different fuel types. For cost, performance, and technology replacement reasons it may prove more difficult to switch away from high-carbon automotive fuels to lower carbon-content or non-carbon automotive fuels.

In Sweden, a tax differential was introduced in 1991 on diesel fuels in order to stimulate the consumption of less polluting fuel oils. From 1992 to 1996, the proportion of "clean" diesel sold in Sweden rose from 1% to 85%, which led to a reduction of more than 75% on average in the sulphur emissions of diesel-driven vehicles [Swedish EPA (1997)]. The UK government has taken steps to encourage the manufacture and consumption of ultra-low sulphur diesel (ULSD), which reduces particulate emissions from diesel vehicles, and allows the introduction of the latest diesel after-treatment devices, such as particulate traps. A 1 pence per litre duty differential in favour of ULSD was introduced in 1997. This was increased to 2 pence per litre in 1998 and to 3 pence per litre in 1999. This policy has resulted in almost the entire diesel market converting to ULSD, ahead of most other European countries.[10] A similar measure has been implemented in Norway. In Finland the excise duty on liquid transport fuels is staggered by grade of petrol and diesel; with lower tax rates applied to low sulphur diesel and reformulated gasoline. This measure has been very effective in changing the composition of fuels used.

In Belgium, the tax differentiation between heavy fuels with a sulphur content below or above 1% induced a decrease in the use of the fuel with the higher sulphur content from 20% of the market in 1994 to less than 1% in 1998. This change has also been due to industrial users switching away from heavy fuel oils to natural gas.

8.3.2. Non-energy tax rate differentials

The Dutch groundwater tax goes some way to reduce the price differential between groundwater and surface water (30% of the water supply), however, groundwater is still cheaper than surface water and therefore incentives to switch supplies are still weak. The groundwater tax sets tax rate differentials between extracted groundwater, and extracted artificially charged groundwater, to provide incentives for increased artificial recharge (using surface water).

Austria, Denmark, and Norway differentiate their respective waste taxes between the efficiency of the waste facility. For example, in Austria and Denmark a lower tax rate is levied on waste delivered to a landfill with methane recovery. Whilst in Norway the waste tax also differentiates between waste streams: a lower tax rate is applied to incinerated waste than landfilled waste, in addition to a lower tax rate on efficient incinerators.

The Danish tax on raw materials exempts recycled materials from the tax. This has generated incentives for the use of recycled material. Similarly environmentally related tax differentials between taxes on beverage containers depending on whether they are part of deposit and refund scheme (re-use), for example in Norway and Finland, generate incentives for re-using beverage containers.

8.4. Improving the environmental effectiveness of taxes

The evidence shows that taxes and tax rate differentiation between substitute products, activities and resources can accelerate market change towards less environmentally harmful products. In Sweden tax differentials favouring lower sulphur diesel not only resulted in lower average sulphur emissions from diesel-driven vehicles, but also created incentives for refineries to sell a "clean" version of light fuel oil, for heating systems as well. Because of the differences in combustion techniques employed in vehicles and heating systems, this practice had no environmental benefit, but caused a substantial loss of revenue to the government. The rules concerning the rate differentiation was hence later changed. This example shows that governments need to tightly define the tax-base in order to prevent any abuse of appropriate environmental incentives.

Environmentally related taxes can be a rather blunt instrument at the level of marginal external costs. The marginal external costs of an activity, for example road transport, will vary by area and population affected, time, and emissions concentration. For example, the health and environmental costs of road transport are likely to be highest in peak flow traffic, on hot summer days, in cities with high population densities. Road pricing, i.e. taxes for road use, could be implemented to create disincentives for road use in high damage areas or time periods.

Tax rates in environmentally related taxes should be based on an assessment of the environmental damage of the product or activity, whilst other policy objectives are also taken into account. Initially, the tax rates of the UK landfill tax were based on an environmental assessment of the impact of different types of waste. However, in 1998 the UK government increased the basic rate of the landfill tax from £8 to £10 per tonne of waste with effect from 1999 and announced a £1 per tonne per year increase until 2004. These increases have altered the purpose of the tax away from internalising estimated external costs, in order to ensure that the UK meets its EU target for reducing the landfilling of biodegradable municipal waste. The new tax rates are environmentally "wrong", however, the rising cost of landfill is expected to make local authorities investigate alternatives to landfill and thereby indirectly the tax will impact on municipal waste. The government is now exploring the option of tradable permits as a complementary measure that would target municipal waste more directly. An alternative strategy to fulfil the EU targets, would be to redesign the current waste tax. For example, households could be made directly subject to the tax, thereby creating incentives for further waste minimisation and composting.

There are means to improve the design of an environmentally related tax. For example, Denmark has altered the design of its SO_2 tax levied on electricity producers' emissions. The previous system was based on electricity produced. However, from 2000, power plants have to pay according to their emissions.

111|

The available evidence shows that environmentally related taxes are often effective policy instruments to reduce pollution and waste and to create incentives for product shifts and resource conservation. Nevertheless, no government undertakes systematic evaluations of the environmental effectiveness of their environmentally related taxation. This may reflect that many of these taxes have newly been introduced, and therefore the impact is not yet known, and it can also be because it is difficult to disentangle the impact of the environmentally related tax from related policies. In addition, it is likely that the environmental awareness effects resulting from environmentally related taxation can be significant for both consumers and producers accelerating the shift to less environmentally harmful products.

It should be noted that no data is available on marginal abatement costs between firms or sectors subject to environmentally related taxation, and therefore there is no documented evidence of the static efficiency of environmentally related taxation. However, EPA (2001) quotes a long list of estimates of potential savings of applying economic incentives to control air pollution, water pollution, solid waste, etc., compared to the costs under "traditional" regulation-based approaches. The ratio of costs between the "traditional" approach and an "incentives-based" approach was in every case larger than 1, and in many cases substantially larger.

There is also only scant information on technology shifts and developments to support the dynamic efficiency argument in favour of economic instruments. It is difficult to measure the impact of environmentally related taxation on dynamic efficiency, in part because of the relatively short time span that environmentally related taxes have been implemented and the relatively low tax rates applied. However, EPA (2001) lists technologies that are said to have been developed, in part, in response to the economic instruments applied under the Clean Air Act.

Taxes also create incentives for changes in production *practice* as well as technology development. For example, in response to the Danish pesticides tax, dose per application has declined, in part due to changes in agricultural management. These secondary benefits may be harder to measure and therefore include in an assessment of a environmentally related tax. The fundamental point is that environmentally related taxation should be based on *environmental criteria, i.e.* the relative damage of substitute products/fuels etc, in order to provide incentives to polluters to switch to less environmentally damaging products. A tax based on such criteria would in itself tend to create incentives for new less environmentally damaging substitutes to be developed (dynamic efficiencies).

NOTES

1. This section is based on OECD (2000a). This study includes information on the economic theory and limitations of elasticities, approaches to estimate price elasticities, and empirical information on demand price elasticities.

2. For example, regulations making it compulsory for service stations to offer unleaded petrol, the introduction of new emission standards for motor vehicles, and the pre-announcement that leaded petrol would be phased-out by a specific date.

3. Data from Ecotec (2000).

4. See HM Treasury (1999a) and (1999b) and DETR (2000). Total projected carbon emissions from the transport sector in the UK in 2010 are 43.3 million tonnes of carbon.

5. A new evaluation of the Norwegian CO_2 taxation is currently undertaken by Statistics Norway for the Ministry of Environment. Results are expected in the spring of 2001.

6. Arbejdsrapport fra Miljøstyrelsen Nr. 96, 1997, Affaldsafgiften 1987-1996.

7. This paragraph is based on Ecotec (2000).

8. This paragraph is based on Ecotec (2000).

9. For a recent review of the literature on price elasticity of water demand, see Nauges and Thomas (2000). Their own estimate for France is -0.22.

10. A similar opportunity now exists for ultra-low sulphur petrol (ULSP). ULSP reduces emissions compared to ordinary petrol and enables the introduction of cleaner vehicle technologies. The government introduced a differential of 1 pence per litre in favour of ULSP relative to unleaded petrol from October 2000.

Chapter 9

TAXING GREENHOUSE GASES: ISSUES AND OPTIONS

9.1. Taxation and the Kyoto Protocol

In December 1997, 160 countries agreed the Kyoto Protocol to the Untied Nations Framework Convention on Climate Change. Once the Protocol enters into force, it establishes legally binding quantitative emission reduction commitments for the industrialised nations (Annex I parties) to achieve by 2008-2012. Crucially, environmentally related taxes could play a key role in fulfilling obligations under the Protocol. According to Article 2, Paragraph 1 *a*)*v*) of the Protocol, all Annex I Parties shall "implement and/or further elaborate policies and measures in accordance with its national circumstances, such as ... progressive reduction or phasing out of market imperfections, fiscal incentives, tax and duty exemptions and subsidies in all greenhouse gas emitting sectors that run counter to the objective of the Convention and apply market instruments." Under Article 2*b*) the Parties shall "share their experience and exchange information on such policies and measures". This report provides such information on OECD Member-country experience with designing and implementing energy/carbon taxation.

The Kyoto Protocol is denominated in a basket of six greenhouse gases converted to CO_2 equivalents (C_{eq}) by a global warming potential index. The potent nature of the non-CO_2 greenhouse gases and relatively low cost mitigation potential, means that efforts to reduce these emissions could contribute a significant proportion of a country's overall greenhouse gas emission reduction target. The underlying trends in emissions differ between the gases. Furthermore, there are large variations in marginal abatement costs across the different gases. By allowing the substitution of abatement of non-CO_2 gases, the Kyoto Protocol, enables efficiency gains to be achieved. It is for this reason, that many OECD countries are interested in mechanisms and policies to reduce the emissions of these gases. For example, environmentally related taxes on waste, as part of waste management policies, also contribute to methane emission reductions.

The OECD Secretariat has previously estimated the costs of fulfilling the Kyoto Protocol requirements [OECD (1999 *b*)] using the GREEN model and assuming only CO_2 emissions could be abated.[1] More recently this model has been adjusted to include methane and nitrous oxide emissions, as well as, carbon dioxide emissions.

9.2. The Kyoto Protocol and the flexible mechanisms

The aggregate target for Annex I countries is to cut greenhouse gas emissions by 5.2% from 1990 levels to the period 2008-2012 on average. This aggregate target may not appear ambitious, however, given economic growth, and no change in policy, emissions would have been much higher in the commitment period than they were in 1990.[2] Emission reduction of this magnitude will require significant policy action, and major structural adjustments in the economies of OECD countries, and other non-Annex I countries. The Protocol incorporates a number of instruments that provide some flexibility to the signatories to meet their commitments:

1. a group of countries can decide to meet their targets collectively;
2. the targets are designated in a basket of greenhouse gases, allowing mitigation flexibility among the gases; and

3. the option to deploy Kyoto mechanisms to meet domestic commitments, including international emissions trading (ET), and two types of project-based emission reduction crediting, joint implementation (JI) and the clean development mechanism (CDM) (see Box 16).

Box 16. Kyoto Protocol flexible mechanisms

Emissions trading allows the marginal abatement costs in different Annex I countries to be equalised by trading emission permits so that emission reductions in one country, where they can be done relatively cheaply, may be counted against the target for another, where emission reductions are more costly. In the process both countries can benefit.

The Kyoto Protocol contains two mechanisms for project-based transfers between countries. While so-called *Joint Implementation* among Annex I countries resembles emission trading in that it leads to transfers of emissions rights, the *Clean Development Mechanism* allows Annex I countries to gain emission rights from investments to cut emissions by developing countries. The latter do not have emission targets and the transfers of emission rights are therefore outside of the Annex I target. The amount of credits available for transfer under both mechanisms have to be made with reference to agreed, project-specific, baselines for emissions.

_____

Source: OECD (1999*b*).

For a number of reasons, there is considerable interest in the flexible mechanisms. First, climate change is an unusual environmental problem:

- there are currently no commercial abatement (end-of-pipe) solutions for the main greenhouse gas, CO_2,[3] and therefore the only option is to avoid emissions at source. For fossil fuel combustion, which is the main source of CO_2 emissions, this is done either through a substitution to fuels with lower or no carbon-content, through a change in technology, or a reduction in energy use more generally; and

- greenhouse gas emissions are uniform pollutants, and therefore the country in which emission reductions are realised is in *scientific* terms irrelevant.

Second, the marginal costs of reducing emissions vary from country to country. A cost-effective pattern of emission reduction, therefore, will not be achieved without trading among Annex I countries. In *economic* terms it is important to have an efficient, least-cost pattern of greenhouse gas reduction within, and between, countries to reduce costs. Differences in marginal costs of mitigation among countries and within countries, creates incentives to utilise the flexible mechanisms in order to lower the cost of achieving targets. However, the final details of these mechanisms, including possible limits on their use, have not yet been finalised. Present IPCC climate change scenarios for the future show that, long term emission reductions will have to be much larger, and will probably have to include developing country emissions, to bring the objective of the Convention into reach.

9.3. Potential for CO_2 taxation in OECD

Few OECD countries have implemented taxes more or less based on, the carbon content of energy; however, most governments have introduced other taxes on energy. "Implicit carbon taxes" are the sum of all taxes on the various energy sources. Implicit carbon taxes vary significantly between fuels and countries Some fuels, those consumed by individuals and typically with relatively inelastic demand, for example petrol and diesel, are heavily taxed in many European countries. In contrast, fuels used by industry are subject to lower or no implicit carbon tax. In all countries, coal (almost exclusively used by industry), the most carbon-intensive fossil fuel, has a low or zero implicit carbon tax. In fact, in Germany and Spain coal is heavily subsidised [Ekins and Speck (1999)]. The substantial discrepancy between implicit carbon taxes by fuel demonstrates the need for reform of tax "structure" [Hoeller and Coppel (1992)]. More significant emission reduction could be achieved at lower total costs if governments reduced rebates and exemptions on certain fuels and certain sectors, *e.g.* through internationally co-ordinated action.

International co-ordination of carbon taxation could reduce the competitive risks and improve the effectiveness of carbon taxation. However, tax co-ordination is a sensitive issue. The EU has been working towards tax harmonisation for all energy products, including electricity, since 1992. The Ecofin Council is still discussing a draft directive issued in 1997. This proposal is for increased minimum taxes levels on all energy products, including electricity and heat, and a staggered introduction of progressively higher tax rates. The slow progress on tax harmonisation, and on the implementation of the Kyoto mechanisms, underlines the difficulties of co-ordinated environmental policy making.

There are a number of conclusions about the potential for CO_2 taxation in OECD countries:

- the long-run sectoral competitiveness obstacle is almost definitely smaller than the energy-intensive sectors often claim, because in many cases[4] these sectors have the most opportunities to fuel-switch to lower carbon fuels and to invest in energy efficiency measures, many of which will be no-regrets responses (cost-effective over the life of the investment). However, short-run problems may be real, yet could be addressed by co-ordinated action (see Section 4.5);

- there is growing evidence of a limited, but positive double dividend following a green tax shift, and increased understanding of the effectiveness of different options of revenue-recycling, *i.e.* the advantages of reducing employers social security contributions (see Section 2.3); and

- stricter emission targets in the future might increase the role of CO_2 (and non-CO_2) taxation.

Therefore a possible policy solution is to shift the focus from automatically protecting affected sectors to one which defines how long such sectors should receive relief. Governments might also look at how to build the capacity of these sectors to respond to price incentives. Over time, governments should plan to phase-out temporary exemptions and rebates in a gradual and predictable manner, with the objective to work towards a cost-effective uniform carbon tax. Another possibility is to pursue, perhaps in parallel, co-ordinated adoption of minimum greenhouse gas taxes.

9.3.1. Additional environmental benefits of CO_2/energy taxation

Climate change models rarely include estimates of the considerable ancillary benefits of CO_2/greenhouse gas taxation that creates incentives to reduce fossil fuel use and to switch to lower carbon-content (cleaner) fuels. In addition to the climate change benefits significant secondary, or ancillary, environmental benefits[5] can be expected from carbon taxation, specifically the reduction in local air pollutants, and resulting damage costs, related to, health expenditures, crop, and infrastructure damage. However it can be difficult to monetise such benefits. A number of studies reviewed by Pearce *et al.* (1996) and Davis *et al.* (2000) have estimated these benefits ranging from $2 per tonne of carbon abated to $500 per tonne.[6] The inclusion of these additional environmental benefits, in a benefit-cost analysis of emission/energy reduction, would offset some of the costs of emission reduction, *i.e.* fuel switching, technology change and output reduction costs.

9.4. The importance of the non-CO_2 greenhouse gases

Carbon dioxide is responsible for over 60% of anthropogenic greenhouse gas emissions. Methane currently contributes 15-20% of the greenhouse effect and nitrous oxide and other gases contribute the remaining 20% of the greenhouse effect.[7] The most important sources of each of the non-CO_2 greenhouse gases in terms of quantities emitted are:

- methane (CH_4) from landfills, enteric fermentation in ruminants, natural gas and oil systems, and coal mining;

- nitrous oxide (N_2O) from fertilisers and industrial processes;

- hydrofluorocarbons (HFCs) used in place of ozone depleting substances (ODS) and HFC-23 as a by-product from production of HCFC-22;

- perfluorocarbons (PFCs) from anode effects during aluminium production; and

- sulphur hexafluoride (SF_6) used in electrical insulators and during magnesium production.

Most modelling of the cost of achieving the Kyoto targets on the global economy, including previous simulations on the OECD's GREEN model, only cover the most important greenhouse gas, CO_2. More recent OECD modelling includes other greenhouse gases. The inclusion of methane and nitrous oxide in the model reduces the necessary abatement relative to the baseline emission. This is because these non-CO_2 emissions are projected to grow more slowly than CO_2 emissions, or to decline, even in the absence of policy action. There are more options for reducing non-CO_2 emissions, than for CO_2 emissions. GREEN results show that the inclusion of the two gases reduces abatement effort by a fifth, to 18% in 2010, as compared with 22%, if only CO_2 is considered.

The inclusion of other greenhouse gases (CH_4 and N_2O) in the analysis reduces the estimated costs of meeting the Kyoto targets, and also alters the pattern of expected emission reduction effort. The role of the agricultural sector in achieving emission reductions increases, whilst the contribution from energy-intensive sectors to total emission reduction declines. The European Union Member states particularly benefit from the inclusion of the two gases in cost estimates, because these emissions are already declining in the absence of climate policy. By contrast, in Japan the inclusion of the two gases in the modelling does little to change baseline emission trends. Finally, the inclusion of N_2O and, in particular, CH_4 emissions reduces the share of OECD country emission in total world emissions from 53% to 47% in 1995, whilst the share of non-Annex I countries increases from 36% to 43%, in the same year.

The flexibility to mitigate across the three greenhouse gases and the use of the Kyoto mechanisms both substantially reduce the marginal cost of emissions abatement. In the scenario where flexibility mechanisms are not used, permit prices are estimated to fall from $150 to $100 per tonne of C_{eq} in 1995 prices with the inclusion of the two non-CO_2 gases. In the scenario where there is unrestricted use of JI and ET, the cost of a permit falls from $90 per tonne of C_{eq} with CO_2 only to $60 when all three gases are considered. Finally, in the scenario with unrestricted use of all flexibility mechanisms (including CDM[8]), the cost of permit is calculated to fall from $9 to $7 per tonne of C_{eq}, with the addition of the two gases. In theory tax rates set at the permit price levels, would produce the same volume of emission reduction. In GDP terms, these costs are reduced to one-tenth of a per cent of GDP. The overall economic costs in terms of GDP are a quarter lower with the inclusion of CH_4 and N_2O.[9]

9.5. Taxing non-CO_2 greenhouse gases[10]

Emissions of non-CO_2 greenhouse gases come from many different sources, each of which presents different challenges when considering taxation and other mitigation options. The feasibility of taxing non-CO_2 gases depends largely on:

- how complicated it is to estimate or measure the emissions;

- the number of taxable events;

- the importance of each emission source in terms of current and expected future emissions; and

- the probable interaction with other policies and measures that may be in place to control the emissions.

9.5.1. Non-CO_2 greenhouse gas sources suitable for taxation

Table 10 summarises the greenhouse gas sources that appear to be most amenable to taxation. These arguments are based on technical requirements, for example ease of measurement, number of polluters, etc. Tax policy issues are not covered in the report. The table includes all of the greenhouse gas sources that warrant consideration for taxation, including those sources where *current* data quality is relatively poor, or high levels of uncertainty exist.

Table 10. **Greenhouse gas sources that are suitable for taxation**

Activity	Quantity of taxable entities	Importance	Ease of measurement/ monitoring
CH_4 from oil and natural gas production	Few (producers)	High	Reasonable
CH_4 from modern landfills	Many	High	Good
CH_4 from underground coal mines	Medium	High	Good (for underground mining
N_2O from fertilisers	Many (purchasers)	High	Poor
HFCs and PFCs used as ODS substitutes	Many (producers or purchasers)	Low but increasing rapidly	Good (complex to get complete accuracy)
JHFCs, PFCs, SF_6 emissions during production of these chemicals	Few	High	Good
SF_6 used in magnesium processes	Few to medium	Low	Good
HFC-23	Few	Medium (being phased out)	Good
N_2O from adipic acid	Few	High (but reducing)	Good
N_2O from nitric acid	Few	High	Good (but site specific)
PFCs from aluminium production	Low	Medium	Good (but site specific)

Source: Reproduced from Tables 2.1, 3.2 and 4.6 of OECD (2000b).

Of the emission sources listed in Table 10, the most relevant candidates for taxation seem to be:

- CH_4 from modern landfills – although it can be difficult to make a "fair" and practicable delimitation versus other landfills;
- CH_4 emissions from natural gas and oil production;
- N_2O from use of fertilisers (with the tax placed at point of production or sale);
- HFCs (and some PFCs) that are used as ODS replacements (with the tax placed at point of production or sales); and
- SF_6 used during magnesium production.

Good quality data on emissions exists, or can be estimated, for the above gases and sources. In addition there are a small number of large companies that are easy to monitor, and therefore taxation is technically viable. For example, it is technically feasible to collect data on CO_2 and CH_4 emissions from the small numbers of oil and gas producers. A differentiated tax, with a higher tax rate for CH_4 would create incentives to flare (producing CO_2), collect, or re-inject CH_4. It is also possible to collect data on the production and sales of HFCs used as ODC replacements, and SF_6 use in magnesium and other processes, and to either tax the product directly, or emissions, through estimated emission rates by process (see Annex IV.1 for more detail).

9.5.2. Non-CO_2 greenhouse gas sources not suited to taxation

There are many sources of greenhouse gases that would be problematic to tax, mainly because of measurement or estimation difficulties. These are summarised in Table 11.

The report suggests that the following important sources of greenhouse gas emission are currently not suitable for taxation:

- CH_4 and N_2O from fuel combustion;
- CH_4 from landfills without methane collection systems installed, natural gas distribution, surface coal mining, enteric fermentation, and rice production;

Table 11. **Greenhouse gas sources that are not suitable for taxation**

Activity	Quantity of taxable entities	Importance	Ease of measurement/ monitoring
CH_4 and N_2O from vehicle fuel combustion	Many	Low	Poor
CH_4 and N_2O from stationary fuel combustion	Many	Reasonable	Poor
CH_4 from old landfills	Many	High	Poor
CH_4 from surface coal mining	Medium	High	Poor
CH_4 from natural gas distribution	Medium	Very high	Poor (for open cast)
CH_4 from enteric fermentation	Many: farmers	High	Poor
CH_4 from livestock production	Many: farmers	Medium	Poor
CH_4 from waste water	Many	Low	Poor
N_2O from sprad of animal waste	Many	Low	Poor
CH_4 and N_2O from manure management	Many	Low	Poor
HFCs, PFCs, and SF_6 used in the semi- conductor industry	Many	High	Uncertain

Source: Reproduced from Tables 2.1, 3.2 and 4.6 of OECD (2000*b*).

- N_2O from agricultural soils and animal waste; and
- HFCs, PFCs, and SF_6 used in semi-conductor manufacturing processes.

These emissions would be difficult to tax because of monitoring problems (*e.g.* old landfills) or expense (*e.g.* surface coal mining) or the difficulty of estimating emissions in different management environments (*e.g.* emissions from livestock and rice cultivation). It is also difficult estimate emissions of HFCs, PFCs, and SF_6 from the semi-conductor industry, as emissions vary with plant utilisation, product type and complexity. Finally, although it is possible to measure CH_4 and N_2O emissions from fuel combustion, these emissions are relatively minor and trending downwards without specific climate change policies (see Annex IV.2 for a more detailed account). Although these emissions may not be suitable for taxation, other policies may be effective in capturing cost-effective mitigation from these sources. For example, the US has had some success in working with farmers, the natural gas industry, and landfill operators to initiate CH_4 capture programmes.

The Norwegian Quota Commission (1999) identified greenhouse gas emission sources suitable for inclusion in a domestic tradable permit scheme. Although the report was written for tradable permits the same principles of measurement and monitoring apply to taxation. The Commission estimates that if all greenhouse gases from all point sources considered technically feasible for regulation by quotas are included in a quota scheme, the system would cover almost 90% of total greenhouse gas emissions (based on Norwegian emission levels in 1997). However, the inclusion of some gases from some sources will require further developments in emission monitoring or estimates. Greenhouse gas emissions from the following sources are not yet considered technical feasible for inclusion in a permit scheme. They are:

- CH_4 and N_2O from combustion;
- CO_2 from agricultural liming and from solvents;
- CH_4 and N_2O from agriculture;
- HFCs/PFCs used as substitutes from CFCs and halons; and
- SF_6 emissions, excepting those from magnesium production.

This list is very similar to that in 9.5.1. Note the inclusion of all point source emissions, *i.e.* emissions from landfills and natural gas distribution. The list also includes CO_2 emissions from liming and solvents (not covered in the OECD study). In the OECD study, HFCs used as ODS substitutes, were described as technically feasible to measure and monitor, and therefore tax (trade). The result is that approximately a tenth of total greenhouse gas emissions in Norway are likely to fall outside of a tax system (or tradable permit system) and would either need to be controlled by other means, or remain unregulated. Depending on the emissions profile in individual countries, a greenhouse gas tax (permit) system could be fairly comprehensive, covering a large proportion of greenhouse gas emissions.

9.5.3. *Interaction with existing policies and measures*

In some cases other policies and measures (or technical solutions) than taxes may be more appropriate mechanisms for reducing the emissions. Some sources of non-CO_2 greenhouse gas emissions are managed through other measures, and others are already declining in the absence of policy measures. It could nevertheless be more cost-effective to replace – or supplement – these measures with taxes. Sources that make a very small contribution to global warming or that are expensive to monitor may not be worth taxing, unless the tax can be added to an existing measure easily. However, for the very long lived gases: PFC, HFC and SF_6, the necessity to find substitutes to avoid significant damage to the atmosphere, supports the use of regulatory measures rather than economic instruments. Research could be undertaken into how taxes on greenhouse gas emissions from various sources interact with existing or planned policies and measures.

9.6. OECD Member country experience with taxing non-CO_2 greenhouse gases

At present there is little OECD country experience with non-CO_2 greenhouse gas taxation. The Czech Republic, Denmark, Hungary, Poland, Sweden, and the US all levy taxes on ODCs (see Box 7). There are no methane taxes recorded in the OECD, but many governments implement waste management/landfill taxes that indirectly impact on CH_4 emissions. Austria applies differentiated waste taxes depending on whether the landfill site collects methane gases, or not. It is also important to note that planning controls and regulations at new landfill sites have improved landfill design, and promoted gas collection, and thus contributed to more effective mitigation of CH_4 emissions. Norway estimates that its waste tax will create incentives for better management of landfill sites, and could reduce methane emissions by between 1 and 1.5 million tonnes.

NOTES

1. The OECD Secretariat has developed a world, multi-region, multi-sector, dynamic applied general equilibrium model named GREEN. The model has been used to derive estimates of the impacts and costs of fulfilling the commitments envisaged under the Kyoto Protocol.

2. Burniaux (2000) calculates that compared to a Business-as-Usual scenario, the reduction in greenhouse emissions required by the Kyoto Protocol from Annex I countries, amounts to some 20% to 30%.

3. Abatement options do, however, exist for other greenhouse gas emissions.

4. Coal and coke is used as a raw material in some metal processes.

5. The term ancillary benefits, indicates impacts that arise *incidental* to mitigation policies.

6. Most studies to date focus on the benefits of reduced health expenditures so these figures may not represent the full range of benefits.

7. UNFCCC website: *http://www.unfccc.de*.

8. There are a number of reasons, discussed in OECD (1999*b*) why the cost saving potential of CDM may not be fully exploited.

9. Three recent reports support these conclusions. Brown *et al.* (1999) show that the inclusion of CH_4 and N_2O emissions reduces the costs of meeting the Kyoto targets by a third, compared to a CO_2-only scenario. Reilly *et al.* (1999) estimate that the inclusion of the other greenhouse gases and carbon sinks may reduce the costs of implementing the Protocol by as much as 40%, whilst Manne and Richels (2000) estimate the cost savings to be greater at 48%.

10. This section is based on OECD (2000*b*), which reviews the different non-CO_2 greenhouse gases covered under the Kyoto Protocol, their significance in terms of emissions and global warming potential, the main emitters, the ease of monitoring emissions, and the feasibility of applying taxes. It should be underlined that the study deals neither with the fiscal implications nor with the economic impact of such taxes.

Chapter 10

GREEN TAX REFORMS: AN ASSESSMENT

When implementing new policy measures, the environmental (and other) objectives of the measure should be clearly stated from the outset. In some cases, the objectives pursued can be conflicting. For instance, policies aiming to lower NO_x emissions can in some cases cause increased greenhouse gas emissions. There can also be conflicts between environmental policy objectives and objectives related to economic development, competitiveness of certain industrial sectors, regional employment possibilities, etc. Often environmentally related taxes can be usefully implemented in the context of policy packages, *i.e.* in combination with other policy instruments, such as voluntary approaches, command and control regulations, and tradable permits. Modifications to existing taxes, for instance on energy, may also be an option, even where environmentally related objectives were not explicitly given when these taxes were introduced. When deciding on a particular measure, each country should carefully review the range of measures that could potentially be used to achieve those objectives. A thorough analysis of the costs and benefits of each approach and an assessment of current practices should be carried out in order to evaluate the relative merits of the alternative measures.

The OECD/EU database on environmentally related taxation and other country-based information provide evidence of where taxes are working, where the problems lie, and where there are no environmentally related taxes, though they might have been expected. An assessment of environmental effectiveness can also include qualitative judgements on whether the tax was more, or less, environmentally effective than had been predicted. For example, the rapid decline in coal burn in the United Kingdom demonstrated the larger than expected (and cheaper than expected) substitution possibilities for electricity generation, whilst a lower than expected response to a household electricity tax, might highlight information, capital and tenure barriers to energy efficiency behaviour and investments.

The main objective of implementing environmentally related taxation is to reduce the consumption and production of polluting products and activities. However, in practice, many governments have implemented environmentally related taxes and channelled the revenues raised to reduce the marginal tax rates of other distortionary taxation, in an attempt to realise additional benefits from the reform. In the future, governments may be able to better target labour tax rate cuts, in order to maximise any employment benefits (the so called "double dividend", see Section 2.3). There is a need for more *ex post* evaluation of the existence of any real-world "double dividend", and for exchange of practical experience.

There are indications of some future developments in environmentally related taxation. For example, motor vehicle tax can in the future be based more on average or actual emissions of some types of pollutants. A number of countries have also introduced a range of packaging taxes designed to reduce waste from this source and to encourage recycling and reuse. Austrian, Danish and Norwegian efforts at developing environmentally related tax differentials between landfills and incinerators, based on the efficiency of the facility and between the different waste disposal options, are interesting policies that other countries may wish to follow. Denmark has introduced a tax differential between petrol sold at stations with, and without, vapour recovery systems, which may herald a new trend, to impact on the delivery of products. Meanwhile, Ireland [see Irish EPA (2000)] is investigating the practical and fiscal implications of taxation of non-CO_2 greenhouse gases.

10.1. Environmental effectiveness

Many environmentally related taxes have been assessed and found to be effective at reducing consumption/production of environmentally damaging products and activities, and contributing to resource protection. Environmentally related taxes introduce an incentive to change behaviour. A measure of the environmental "effectiveness" of a tax is the price elasticity of demand (see Section 8.1). Although many environmentally harmful activities and products are relatively inelastically demanded, for example energy and private transportation, significant reductions in the consumption and production of the polluting good/activity can be expected after the implementation of a tax. Environmentally related taxation can be used to accelerate the exit of products from the market, for example SO_2 taxation (high sulphur-content fuels) in Sweden, Norway and Finland and taxation on chlorinated solvents in Denmark. Even before actual implementation, the "threat" of, or the practical preparation of, a new tax (or a re-alignment of tax rates in existing taxes) can cause producers and users/consumers to start changing their behaviour.

10.1.1. *Tax-bases, tax rates and tax rate differentials*

Implementing an environmentally related tax requires careful consideration of what the tax base should be, and how to define it, to avoid any unwanted and unforeseen environmental or economic side effects. For many environmentally related taxes included in the database, the tax-bases are fairly simple to define, for example electricity taxes in terms of kWh consumed, petrol taxes in litres and included in the pump price, and water supply taxes charged per m^3 of metered water. The database also shows that the tax-bases of some taxes are more complicated, for example packaging taxes that are differentiated by material used and by product size, or weight. Sometimes a chosen delimitation can prove sub-optimal; for example the tax-base can be too narrowly defined. This can encourage non-environmentally related behavioural change, or results in the passing up of opportunities to change behaviour. For example, landfill taxes provide limited incentives to reduce municipal waste generation, as consumers are not directly subject to the tax. In other cases it may be difficult to define the tax base given lack of information about the different hazards products pose to human health and the environment, and therefore the tax bases diverge between countries. For example, there are three tax bases for pesticides, based on: quantitative ingredient – Sweden, area dose – Norway, and retail price – Denmark.

The determination of environmentally related tax rates, and tax rate differentials, impacts on the environmental effectiveness of the tax. In a few cases governments have based tax rates, and tax rate differentials, on an explicit environmental assessment of the absolute, or relative, environmental damage caused by the product/activities, or substitute products/activities. In these instances, the tax rate internalises the pollution externalities caused by the product, or activity, and creates incentives to reallocate resources and abatement costs according to the new "proper" prices. An example is the UK landfill tax, where the rates for the different waste streams originally were determined by an environmental assessment of the relative environmental damage caused. However, recent changes to the tax, in particular the step-wise increase in rates over the period 2000 to 2005, are not based on an environmental assessment, but rather have been set in order to reach European Union targets on the landfilling of biodegradable municipal waste. In situations where the demand elasticities are low (demand is inelastic), tax rates can be set too low to have a significant impact on an environmentally damaging activity or product. This is, for example, the case concerning the Swedish pesticides tax (see Section 8.2.8).

Environmentally related taxation differentials can have a significant impact on demand for substitute activities and products. Many OECD countries have successfully used such tax differentials to phase out the production and consumption of environmentally more harmful products, for example leaded and high sulphur-content fuels. Tax rate differentials also exist between alternative activities, for example in Austria, Denmark and Norway taxes on waste are differentiated between waste disposal options, *i.e.* incineration and landfill and between the efficiency of the facility, *i.e.* between landfills with and without methane gas recovery (see Section 8.3.2). Other tax rate differentials create incentives for new behaviour, for example lower taxes levied on recycled beverage containers, or for beverage containers being part of a deposit and refund system compared to other beverage containers, creates incentives for recycling and reuse. However, if rate differentials are set too low, a switch in behaviour is unlikely to occur. For example, in the Netherlands one objective of the groundwater tax is to create incentives to switch to surface water supplies. However, the tax rate is too low to create such incentives, but the groundwater tax itself does generate incentives for artificial recharge of aquifers using surface waters (see Section 8.3.2).

10.1.2. *Policy packages and the time horizon*

Many environmentally related taxes are introduced as part of a policy package and therefore it can be difficult to isolate the impact of the tax incentive. In addition, a lack of data on measured pollutants and abatement costs, in part because many environmentally related taxes are relatively recent, can hamper evaluations of specific taxes. In spite of these difficulties, some environmentally related taxes have been evaluated. For example, an assessment of the Danish energy policy package introduced in 1995 calculated the emission reduction achieved by taxes and by other measures: the total package is expected to reduce CO_2 emissions by 3.8%, of which 2 percentage points is attributable to taxation [Danish Government (1999a)].

One of the advantages of environmentally related taxes is that they provide on-going incentives for pollution abatement, providing signals that influence consumer choice, and for structural adjustments in the economy (see Section 1.4). These longer-term impacts of environmentally related taxes can be significant. The time horizon of an assessment should be chosen to capture the dynamic efficiency effects of the economic instrument. Measuring dynamic efficiency effects requires a broad assessment of the impact of the tax on substitute products and activities, patterns of consumption, abatement technology, and management practices. It is important to keep in mind that most macroeconomic models that are used in policy evaluations, *e.g.* to simulate impacts of alternative policies, by default will assume that technological development is unaffected by the policies chosen. This can, in isolation, cause the impacts of a given instrument to be under-estimated.

There are examples of comprehensive assessments, and they demonstrate that a wide perspective is needed in order to capture all of the benefits resulting from the tax incentive. Statistics Denmark, in assessing the impact of the tax on water supply, undertook a survey in 1999 of households, and concluded that around half of those households surveyed had *invested* in water saving appliances. Furthermore, the tax created incentives for better *management* by the water companies in terms of reducing leakage rates. Other examples are the CO_2 tax on Norwegian offshore oil and gas exploration, that has been credited with reduced emissions per unit of oil extracted, and the Swedish tax on hydrocarbons and NO_x emissions, levied on domestic air traffic in 1989 and abandoned in 1997. This tax created incentives for improved engine design that reduced HC emissions in the domestically used airplane, the Fokker F28, by 90% [Brännlund (1999)]. It is important that such longer-term impacts (benefits) be included in an assessment of environmentally related taxes, and thereby improve the benefit-cost analysis of such taxation.

10.1.3. *Competitiveness related exemptions and rebates*

Environmentally related taxation is often implemented with exemptions and/or rebates to certain products, or sectors, in order to reduce the cost impact of the taxation, and related competitive concerns.[*] Often the most polluting sectors and products, precisely those that would pay the most tax, are exempt or receive rebates from environmentally related taxation. For example, most OECD countries that levy taxes on energy use, do not tax coal (see Figure 6) even though coal is the most carbon-intensive fuel, and is responsible for a number of other air pollutants. Most OECD countries also

---

[*] Certain competitiveness-related exemptions have an environmental justification. This is for instance the case with exemptions in electricity taxes for electricity generated by renewable energy sources, like wind-mills, etc. – granted in order to compensate cost disadvantages these sources currently have compared to other energy sources.

exempt or rebate energy-intensive industry, agriculture, fisheries, aviation, etc., from these taxes. The outcome of such provisions is that a major proportion of emissions lies outside the incentive effect of the tax, thus reducing its environmental effectiveness.

Pre-announcing the introduction of environmentally related taxes and tax rate increases, and a *gradual* reduction or phasing out of rebates and exemptions, are two policy options that could make taxes more environmentally and economically effective, while also addressing competitiveness concerns.

Countries would also benefit from exploring better integration of environmentally motivated reforms of their fiscal systems with broader fiscal reforms. It is the combined effects of these reforms that will determine the impacts on sectoral and nation-wide competitiveness. Possible negative competitiveness impacts on some sectors from the environmentally related part of a broader reform might thus be reduced. And while some sectors may face a net loss in competitiveness if countries expand environmentally related taxation unilaterally, other, more environmentally benign, sectors of the economy could improve their competitiveness, *inter alia* depending on how revenues generated in the reform are redistributed.

When considering the competitiveness impacts of environmentally related taxes, it should be kept in mind that any alternative policy instrument used to reduce environmental problems, such as regulations, would also affect firms' costs and impact on the competitiveness position of individual sectors and the country as a whole. By enhancing the economic efficiency by which a given target is reached, properly designed environmentally related taxes will help minimise adverse effects on competitiveness nation-wide.

10.1.4. *Income (re)distribution related exemptions and rebates*

Income distribution issues also impact on the design of environmentally related taxation, including energy/CO_2 taxation, because of concerns that such taxes are income regressive. However, few assessments of the income (re)distributive effects of environmentally related taxation include the wider benefits of such tax packages, for example associated employment benefits resulting from any tax shifting, or the distribution of environmental benefits following the implementation of the tax. Therefore, current evaluations can give a biased view of the income distributive impacts of environmentally related taxation.

Governments have responded to income distribution concerns in two main ways: through mitigation measures and compensation measures. An example of the mitigation approach is the low VAT rate on energy use in households in the United Kingdom, and the exemption of such usage from the new "Climate change levy". The incentive effect a broader energy tax would have had is thus foregone, and the overall environmental effectiveness of the tax is reduced. Generally, a compensation approach would be preferable from an environmental point of view. Here the price signals are improved through appropriate taxes, while those most negatively affected receive compensation through reductions in other taxes, increases in incomes transfers, etc.

10.2. Cost-effectiveness of environmentally related taxation

Although many existing environmentally related taxes implemented in the OECD Member countries contribute to environmental improvements, they are often implemented in a cost-*ineffective* manner. They seldom apply equally across all polluters, in fact the most polluting products and firms are often exempted from the tax or pay a lower rate than others.

This means that some sectors adapt to relatively high tax rates, and measures taken in these sectors to reduce energy use/emissions can be significantly more costly than measures that could have undertaken in other sectors. The tax therefore fails to equalise marginal abatement costs between sectors (which underlies the static efficiency argument of environmentally related taxes) – the pattern of emission reduction undertaken will be inefficient. (See Table 9 for an illustrated example from Germany.)

To date, environmentally related taxes currently imposed by OECD countries have not been identified as causing significant reductions in the competitiveness of any sector. This is consistent with research on economic performance that shows that skills and capital investment largely determine sectoral competitiveness. Also, different sectors within countries differ in terms of their exposure to international trade and competition. The finding is also not surprising given the numerous forms of exemptions and rebates currently granted to business.

Blanket exemptions for polluting products along with rebates for heavy polluting industries can significantly reduce the effectiveness of environmentally related taxes in curbing pollution. Such provisions can also reduce the incentives for developing and introducing new technologies. Consideration might be given to a dual (two-tier) rate structure, rather than the use of full exemptions, with lower rates for the more internationally exposed sectors. The negative environmental effect of exemptions and rate reductions can also be limited by ensuring that exempted firms sign up to stringent mitigation measures. Furthermore, in instances where exemptions and rebates are currently given for competitiveness reasons, countries examining revenue recycling as an option should consider imposing additional taxes on industry, while introducing innovative methods to channel part of the tax revenues back to industry in such a way that marginal abatement incentives are maintained.

In some countries, there is also scope for improving the design of any remaining exemptions and refund mechanisms, to ensure that they are properly targeted to achieve their stated objectives. Careful design and targeting would reduce the economic costs of achieving a given environmental target, including obligations of countries under the Kyoto Protocol.

One way to address international competitiveness concerns is for countries to share information, experiences and best practices as regards possible options and opportunities for expanding the application of environmentally related taxes. Countries concerned with competitiveness implications of adjusting certain environmentally related taxes on a unilateral basis may also wish to consider possible concerted policy options and changes, decided and implemented at the national level, but within a framework which provides for a multilateral dialogue. The OECD provides a unique forum to facilitate such policy discussions, bringing together tax and environment experts from the governments of 30 developed countries while also providing an extensive outreach programme which now covers over 60 non-member countries.

Annex I

BASIC ECONOMIC ANALYSIS OF "FIRST-ROUND" EFFECTS OF INTRODUCING A CARBON TAX

This annex analyses the "first-round' economic impact of introducing a carbon tax. We first consider the introduction of the tax under monopolistic conditions, and then under competitive conditions.

A.1.1. Imposition of a Carbon Tax Under Monopolistic Conditions

For a given amount of output at the level of the firm, the impact of the tax on cost would depend on the existing production structure, the quantity of fossil fuels consumed, and the carbon tax rate. In general, the immediate effect of a carbon tax would be on production costs measured after-tax, with a shifting up of marginal and average cost curves of the affected firms (*i.e.*, higher marginal and average production costs at each level of output). The impact of these cost shifts on price, output at the level of the firm, and industry output, depends on the market structure of the particular sector.

Where the domestic market is protected from foreign competition or where domestic firms are price-setters on international markets by virtue of special firm characteristics or assets – so that a small number of firms dominate the sector, setting output so as to maximise economic profits – the effect of the introduction of a carbon tax would be an increase in output prices accompanied by output reductions (as opposed to plant closures.)

Figure A.1.1 considers the case of a carbon tax imposed fuels consumed by a monopoly industry. The monopolist produces output level *q*0 at price *p*0 prior to the introduction of the tax. The imposition of the carbon tax increases the long run average and marginal production cost schedules from AC0 to AC1, and MC0 to MC1. The amount of the upward shift in AC and MC would depend on the chosen carbon tax rate, and would also be influenced by the share

Figure A.1.1. **Illustrative impact of carbon tax on monopolist**

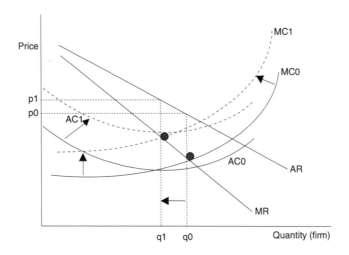

129

of fossil fuels in the monopolist's total cost of production. The effect of the rise in cost curves is to reduce output to $q1$ and to raise price to $p1$.[*]

The increase in the output price means that some part of the burden of the tax is shifted onto consumers of the monopolist's output, with a larger tax burden shift (*i.e.*, a larger price increase) the more inelastic is output demand. Part of the burden of the tax would also fall onto labour where job losses and/or wage reductions result from the scaling back of output.

In the long run, the post-tax cost, output and price structure would depend on the monopolist's ability and profit incentive to substitute away from the taxed factor in favour of untaxed factors that could be used in the production process. Given the existence of pure economic rents following the introduction of the tax, the incentive to invest in R&D to avoid the carbon tax might be less than what one would observe under more competitive market conditions.

A.1.2. Imposition of a Carbon Tax Under Competitive Conditions

Under competitive output markets with output prices fixed in world markets, say at p^*, a carbon tax would result in post-tax operating losses, assuming zero economic profits prior to the introduction of the carbon tax. This case is illustrated below in A.1.2, where the introduction of the carbon tax results in an upward shift of the representative firm's average and marginal cost schedule, and an upward shift of the short-run industry supply schedule as shown in the right-hand diagram. The initial response to the increased production cost is a reduction in output, indicated in Figure 8, from $q0$ to $q1(SR)$ with the new short-run (SR) equilibrium established where the world output price p^* meets the new marginal cost schedule MC1. At this output level, price lies below average cost, implying that the firm is generating economic losses (*i.e.*, total gross revenues are less than total costs), with losses shown by the shaded box.

The reduction in output by firms in the short run causes output of the domestic industry to fall to Q1(SR), with the difference in domestic supply and demand in the amount of (Q0-Q1(SR)) made up by imports. The example assumes that the carbon tax does not apply to imports, given the administrative difficulty in establishing the fossil fuel content of imported goods (*i.e.*, the amount of fossil fuels used in foreign production.)

Figure A.1.2. **Illustrative impact of carbon tax on perfectly competitive firm**

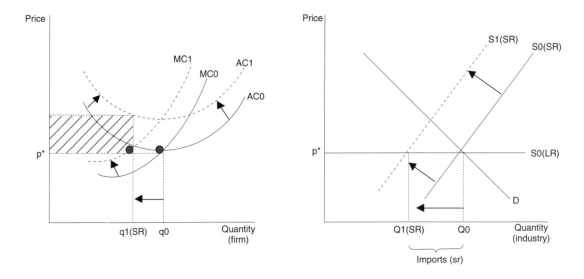

---

[*] The monopolist's profit-maximising decision can be expressed as follows: $\max_q \Pi = [p(q)q - c(q)\lambda(1 + \tau)](1 - u)$ where Π denotes economic profit, τ denotes the carbon tax rate set on fossil fuel consumed, u denotes the corporate income tax rate, output price (p) is a declining function of the level of output (q), and c(q) summarises the firm's cost function assumed to be a linear function of output. The factor input variable λ gives the amount of fossil fuel consumed as a fixed percentage of total production cost. Differentiating with respect to q gives the following first-order condition maximising profit: MR = MC where $MR = p(1 + \varepsilon)$ and $MC = c'(q)\lambda(1 + \tau)$, where ε denotes the price elasticity $(\partial p/\partial q)(q/p)$ and $c'(q) = (\partial c(q)/\partial q)$ gives pre-tax marginal cost. The introduction or increase of the carbon tax increases marginal costs, implying a new equilibrium with higher marginal revenues realised at a lower output level and higher output price.

Over time, and in the absence of technological change, the realisation of economic losses would lead to plant closures. Plant closures (fewer firms) would be represented by furthering shifting over time of the short-run supply schedule S(SR), in the limit reaching the point where firm and industry output has fallen to zero, and domestic demand at the world price, given by Q0, is met by imports.

Plant closures could be minimised where firms are able to adopt technologies allowing for a substitution away from fossil fuels to avoid the factor tax. Technological change that avoids the carbon tax would lower tax-inclusive production costs over a range of output levels (as represented by a shifting down of marginal and average cost curves), tending to eliminate economic losses on account of the tax.

Annex II

THE CASE OF CO-ORDINATED IMPLEMENTATION OF A CARBON TAX

With co-ordinated implementation of a carbon tax across all countries, so that all firms in a given industry regardless of the country of production face the same uniform carbon tax (implying increased production costs for all suppliers of a given output produced using similar technologies and factor inputs), the domestic industry and world (aggregate) supply schedules would rise, implying an increase in the world output price. With higher prices, international demand for the product would fall, but the burden of the tax would be shared across a broader base (the burden of the tax would not fall on domestic producers, consumers and labour alone) and fairer competition would be observed.

Figure A.2.1 considers the impact on domestic firms in an energy-intensive, competitive market following the introduction of a uniform carbon tax imposed on all countries on a harmonised basis. As discussed in the previous annex, the tax increases the production costs of the domestic firms, as illustrated by the shifting up of the average and marginal cost curves. However, because the tax has a similar effect on firms producing in other countries, the world market supply curve shifts up. The increase in the world price avoids the economic losses that would otherwise occur.

The price increase has the intended effect of reducing domestic and world demand, with fewer domestic firms required to meet the reduced domestic demand. However, while domestic supply does fall, it is not eliminated or as significantly reduced (even before considering the dynamic efficiency effects) as was shown to be the case in Figure 8 under the unilateral carbon tax adoption scenario. The reason is because the burden of the tax is now spread, with individuals in all countries sharing the burden of the tax.

Figure A.2.1. **Harmonised adoption of carbon tax: illustrative effects**

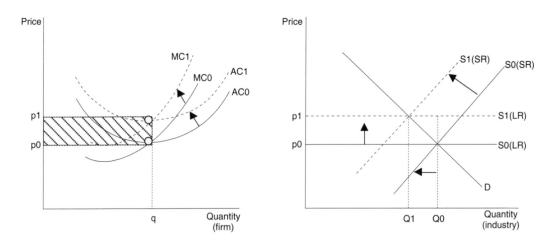

Annex III
ODC TAXATION IN THE US

For details on the implementation of these taxes, see Box 7 and Section 4.3.6.

Table A.3.1.　**Ozone-depleting chemical taxation in the US**

Post-1989 ODCs	Tax ($ per pound) in 2000
CFC-11	7.60
CFC-12	7.60
CFC-113	6.08
CFC-114	7.60
CFC-115	4.56
Halon-1211	22.80
Halon-1301	76.00
Halon-2402	45.60
Post-1990 ODCs	
Carbon tetrachloride	8.36
Methyl chloroform	0.76
CFC-13, CFC-111, CFC-112, and CFC-211 through CFC-217	7.60

Source:　IRS (2000).

Table A.3.2.　**Tax on floor stocks of ODCs**

ODCs	Tax ($ per pound) in 2000
CFC-11	0.45
CFC-12	0.45
CFC-113	0.36
CFC-114	0.45
CFC-115	0.27
Halon-1211	1.35
Halon-1301	4.50
Halon-2402	2.70
Carbon tetrachloride	0.495
Methyl chloroform	0.045
CFC-13, CFC-111, CFC-112, and CFC-211 through CFC-217	0.45

Source:　IRS (2000).

Annex IV

NON-CO$_2$ GREENHOUSE GAS TAXATION

IV.1. Non-CO$_2$ gas sources that are technically feasible to tax

The following section provides more detailed information on the non-CO$_2$ greenhouse gases that are easiest to tax, for reasons of measurement, monitoring, and emission source.

CH$_4$ *from oil and gas production*

CH$_4$ is emitted during natural gas and oil production and can either be vented as CH$_4$, combusted (flared), or re-injected into the oil/gas well (which can improve productivity). Flaring the CH$_4$ emissions converts the CH$_4$ to CO$_2$, which has a much lower global warming potential than CH$_4$. Venting activities are an important source of CH$_4$, and the recent trend is for slight emissions growth. The IEA has estimated that it may be possible to prevent over 80 per cent of current emissions from the oil and gas industry globally by the year 2010, and that 45 per cent of the emissions from this sector could be avoided at little or no net cost.

It is technically feasible to gather good quality data on emissions from oil and gas production. There are a small number of very large companies that produce oil and gas and their emissions are relatively easy to monitor. A tax could be placed on both CO$_2$ and CH$_4$ emissions from oil and gas production, with a higher tax on CH$_4$. Producers would then have an incentive to flare, collect where possible, or re-inject the CH$_4$ emissions.

CH$_4$ *from modern landfills*

The anaerobic decomposition of waste in landfills is a major source of CH$_4$. The amount of CH$_4$ that is generated from landfills depends on the quantity and composition of the waste but also on the type of landfill. Modern landfills typically include gas collection facilities. It is feasible to apply a flow meter to the pipes and measure the amount of gas that is collected. Tax credits could be issued to landfill operators for gas that is collected and used as an energy source, and a lower tax rate could be applied to gas that is flared and so emitted to the atmosphere as CO$_2$.

CH$_4$ *from underground coal mines*

Coal mining is an important source of emissions. It would be feasible to tax to CH$_4$ emissions from underground coal mines, where the CH$_4$ that is released through venting systems can be collected or monitored relatively easily. However, a reduction in CH$_4$ emissions from underground coal mines is likely in OECD countries as a result of the increasing liberalisation of energy markets, leading to the removal of subsidies, and measures directed at the control of CO$_2$ emissions from fossil fuel energy, such as energy taxes. It may therefore not be necessary to tax CH$_4$ emissions from this source. However, in other areas of the world taxation of emissions from coal mining could create incentives to collect and/or flare methane.

N$_2$O *from fertilisers*

N$_2$O emissions from the use of fertiliser in agriculture vary depending on a number of factors (farm management practices, weather, and type of crop) so it would be difficult to tax these emissions directly. However emissions from fertiliser use are significant and the recent trend is for slight emissions growth, therefore it is important to create incentives to reduce emissions from this source. It would be possible to place a tax on sales of fertiliser as a proxy for emissions. Data on fertiliser sales are readily available. The tax could be differentiated so that controlled-release fertilisers (which are used more efficiently by plants) incur a lower tax. The tax could be combined with best practice guidelines and education programmes on crop management practices that release less N$_2$O.

HFCs *used as ODS replacements*

Production of HFCs (primarily used as ODS replacements) could be monitored either from manufacturer supplied data (this could be problematic because of commercial confidentiality) or from sales data. A tax could be placed on HFC output either on the manufacturers directly or on sales, and could be differentiated to reflect the different global warming potential of the substances. In addition, simplifying assumptions would have to be made about the release of these gases to the atmosphere (consumption or use of these chemicals could be taken to be equal to emissions).

SF_6 use in magnesium and other processes (except semi-conductor manufacture)

SF_6 emissions from the magnesium industry appear to be a good candidate for taxation. SF_6 consumption can be easily measured and no significant conversion or destruction of SF_6 occurs in magnesium casting processes, so emissions from the magnesium industry can be taken as being equal to consumption of SF_6. The usage rate of SF_6 varies widely from company to company and between types of processes so emission factors would have to be gathered at the plant level. There are different tracking techniques that can be used by companies to record annual consumption and most companies already collect this data. In addition there are only a handful of primary magnesium producers and magnesium recyclers to monitor, although die casters are more numerous but still possible to monitor.

The magnesium industry is, however, projected to have the smallest growth rate of all SF_6 emitting sources. The largest growth in emissions is expected to come from the manufacture of products such as tennis balls, sporting shoes, and electrical products. Monitoring SF_6 emissions from these products is difficult, but the sale of chemicals to these product manufacturers could be used as a proxy for emissions. A tax could be paid by producers of SF_6 or by consumers such as magnesium producers, electricity distribution companies, and tennis ball manufacturers. Data on production and sales of SF_6 would have to be collected from producers.

IV.2. Non-CO_2 gas sources that are less well suited to taxation

CH_4 and N_2O emissions from fossil fuel combustion

A CH_4 and N_2O component could be added to existing fuel or energy taxes, but fossil fuel combustion is a small source of these gases and measurement of the emissions is imprecise.

CH_4 from older landfills, surface coal mining and gas distribution

Emissions from older landfills with no CH_4 recovery facilities are less amenable to monitoring and therefore to taxation. Measurement of CH_4 emissions from surface mining is technically difficult and expensive – it would require site-by-site measurements. Although it is technically feasible to make substantial reductions in CH_4 emissions from natural gas distribution, it is difficult to measure emissions from long stretches of pipeline and therefore these systems are not easy to tax. Other policy instruments could be used to limit such emissions.

CH_4 emissions from livestock and rice cultivation

Taxation is also not an appropriate tool for addressing CH_4 emissions from livestock due to the difficulty of measuring CH_4 emissions accurately and the cost of monitoring emissions from a large number of farms. N_2O from livestock waste has similar measurement difficulties. CH_4 emissions from rice cultivation also have measurement difficulties. Emission estimates would have to take into account different water management regimes, the amount and type of organic matter, and the specific conditions of continuous flooding.

HFCs, PFCs, and SF_6 from the semi-conductor industry

It is difficult to estimate emissions of HFCs, PFCs, and SF_6 from the semi-conductor industry as emissions vary with plant utilisation, product type and complexity.

Other industrial greenhouse gas sources

Emissions of HFC-23 from HCFC-22 production are expected to decline in parallel with the phase out of HCFC-22 but taxing these emissions (or taxing HCFC-22 production itself) may accelerate ODS phase out.

N_2O from adipic acid manufacture could have been a candidate for taxation but huge (95 per cent) reductions are occurring in emissions of N_2O from adipic acid due to a technical change that is now best practice so the importance of emissions from this source has been dramatically reduced.

Taxing N_2O from nitric acid production may be an option, as it is an important source of emissions with relatively few taxable events and there is scope for emissions reduction. Furthermore many nitric acid production facilities are between 20 and 30 years old, so there are opportunities to update emissions control technologies or install new ones. However monitoring or measuring the emissions would require plant by plant inspection. Similarly, taxing PFCs from the anode effects during aluminium production would have relatively few taxable entities, but would require plant specific emission measurements.

BIBLIOGRAPHY

Adams, J. (1997),
"Environmental Policy and Competitiveness in a Global Economy: Conceptual Issues and a Review of the Empirical Evidence" in *Globalisation and Environment: Preliminary Perspectives*, OECD, Paris.

Alatalo (1998),
Hiilidioksidiveron kaksoishyötyvaikutus, ETLA series B 141.

Andersen, M.S. (1998),
"Assessing the Effectiveness of Denmark's Waste Tax", *Environment*, May 1998.

Andersen, M. S. (1999)
"Governance by green taxes: implementing clean water policies in Europe 1970-1990", *Environmental Economics and Policy Studies* (1999) 2:39-63.

Anderson, R.C., Lohof, A.Q., Carlin, A. (1997),
"The United States Experience with Economic Incentives in Pollution Control Policy", Environmental Law Institute and US EPA, Washington DC.

Ballard, C.L. and Medema S.G. (1993),
"The marginal efficiency effects of taxes and subsidies in the presence of externalities", Journal of Public Economics, 52, No. 2, pp 199-216.

Baranzini A. *et al.* (2000),
A *future for carbon taxes*, Ecological Economics, 32, (2000) 395-412.

Barde, J.P., (1997)
"Economic instruments for environmental protection: experience in OECD countries", in Applying Market-Based Instruments to Environmental Policies in China and OECD Countries. OECD, Paris, pp. 31-58.

Barde, J. P. (2000),
"Environmental policy and policy instruments", in Folmer, H. and Gabel, H. L. (ed.) Principles of Environmental and Resource Economics: A guide for students and decision-makers, Second Edition. Edward Elgar, pp157-201.

Barker and Köhler (1998),
Equity and Ecotax Reform in the EU: Achieving a 10 per cent Reduction in CO_2 Emissions Using Excise Duties, *Fiscal Studies*, Vol. 19, No. 4.

Baron, R. (1996),
Economic/Fiscal Instruments: Taxation (*i.e.* Carbon/Energy). Policies and Measures for Common Action Working Paper, Annex I Expert Group on the UN FCCC.

Birol, Fatih, and Jan Horst Keppler (2000),
Markets and Energy Efficiency Policy: An Economic Approach in Energy Prices and Taxes, first quarter 2000, IEA, Paris.

Bjørner and Jensen (2000),
Industrial Energy Demand and the Effect of Taxes, Agreements and Subsidies. Institute of Local Government Studies, Denmark. Available at *http://www.akf.dk*.

Böhringer, C., and Rutherford, T., F., (1997),
Carbon taxes with exemptions in an open economy: a general equilibrium analysis of the German tax initiative. Journal of Environmental Economics and Management, 32, 189-203.

Böhringer, C., M. Ferris and T.F. Rutherford (1997),
Alternative CO_2 abatement strategies for the Euroepan Union. In: "Economic Aspects of Environmental Policy Making in a Federal State", (J. Braden and S. Proost, Eds.), Edgar Elgar (1997).

Bosquet, B. (2000),
Environmental tax reform: does it work? A survey of the empirical evidence. Journal of Ecological Economics, 34, 19-32.

Braathen, N.A. (2000),
"The OECD/EU Database on EnvironmentallyRelated Taxes". Paper for the conference "Supporting a Sustainable Future: Making Dollars and Sense", Vancouver, Canada, 11-13.12.2000. Available at *http://www.ec.gc.ca/eco-n-ference/*.

Brännlund, R. (1999),
Green tax reforms: some experience from Sweden. In: Schlegelmilch, K. (ed.), 1999. Green Budget Reform in European Countries at the Forefront. Springer, Berlin, pp. 67-91.

Brechling, V. and Smith, S. (1994),
Household energy efficiency in the UK. Fiscal Studies, 15(2), May 1994, pp. 44-56.

Brown, S., D. Kennedy, D. Polidano, K. Woffenden, K. Jakeman, G. Graham, F. Jotzo and B.S. Fisher (1999),
"Economic impacts of the Kyoto Protocol: Accounting for the three major greenhouse gases", Australian Bureau of Agricultural and Resource Economics (ABARE), Research Report 99.6, Canberra.

Burniaux, Jean-Marc (2000),
A Multi-Gas Assessment Of The Kyoto Protoco. Economics Department Working Papers No. 270, OECD, Paris. Available at *http://www.oecd.org/eco/wp/onlinewp.htm#2000*.

Bye, B. and Nyborg, K. (1999),
The welfare effects of carbon policies: grandfathered quotas versus differentiated taxes, Discussion Papers No. 261, October 1999, Statistics Norway, Research Department.

Christiansen, G.B., Tietenberg, T.H. (1985),
Distributional and macroeconomic aspects of environmental policy. In: Kneese, A.V., Sweeney, J.L., (Eds.), Handbook of Natural Resource and Energy Economics. Elsevier, Amsterdam, pp. 345-393.

Clemmesen, F. (1995),
Grøn vaekst, pp. 101-128, Arbejdsbevaegelsens Erhversråd, Copenhagen.

Cook, E. (1996),
Ozone protection in the US: *elements of success.* World Resources Institute, Washington.

Danish Environmental Protection Agency (2000),
Economic Instruments in Environmental Protection in Denmark, Copenhagen.

Danish Government (1999a),
Evaluering af gronne afgifter og erhvervene (Evaluation of Green Taxes and Trade Industry), Copenhagen. In Danish. Available at: *http://147.29.40.164/gronne/index.htm*

Danish Government (1999b),
Note on the Danish Pesticide Tax. Copenhagen.

Danish Ministry of Taxation (1998),
Energy Taxes: The Danish Model. Copenhagen.

Davis D.L., Krupnick A., and McGlynn G. (2000),
Ancillary Benefits and costs of greenhouse gas mitigation: An overview. "Ancillary Benefits and Costs of Greenhouse Gas Mitigation" workshop.

DETR (1999),
The Environmental Appraisal of the Fuel Duty Escalator, Memorandum, Department of the Environment, Transport and the Regions, London. Available at *http://www.parliament.the-stationery-office.co.uk/pa/cm199899/cmselect/cmenvaud/326/326ap01.htm*.

DETR (2000),
Climate Change – The UK *programme.* Department of the Environment, Transport and the Regions, London *http://www.environment.detr.gov.uk/climatechange/cm4913/index.htm*.

DRI (1997),
"Effects of Phasing Out Coal Subsidies in OECD Countries", in OECD (1997c), pp 101-105.

ECMT (1998),
Efficient Transport for Europe, European Conference of Ministers of Transport, Paris.

ECMT (2000),
Efficient Transport Taxes and Charges. European Conference of Ministers of Transport, Paris.

ECOTEC (2000),
Study on the Economic and Environmental Implications of the Use of Environmental Taxes and Charges in the European Union and its Member States, Interim Report, April 2000.

EEA (1996),
Environmental Taxes: Implementation and environmental effectiveness. Summary. European Environmental Agency. Copenhagen.

EEA (2000),
　　Environmental taxes: recent developments in tools for integration. Environmental issues series No. 18. European Environmental Agency. Copenhagen. Available at *http://reports.eea.eu.int:80/Environmental_Issues_No_18/.*

EIEP (2000),
　　The carbon tax to reduce GHGs emission. Report to the Study Group on Economic Instruments in Environmental Policies.

EIM/Haskoning (1999),
　　Study on a European Union wide framework for environmental levies on pesticides. Zoetermeer.

Ekins and Speck (1998a),
　　The Impacts of Environmental Policy on Competitiveness: Theory and Evidence in Barker and Köhler (eds.): International Competitiveness and Environmental Policies, Edward Elgar.

Ekins, P., and Speck, S. (1998b),
　　Database on Environmental taxes in the European Union member state, plus Norway and Switzerland: Evaluation of environmental effects of environmental taxes. Final Report (contract number B4-304/97/000791/ MAR/B1). European Commission.

Ekins, P., and Speck, S. (1999),
　　Competitiveness and Exemptions from Environmental Taxes in Europe. Environmental and Resource Economics, 13: 369-399.

EPA (2001),
　　The United States Experience with Economic Incentives for Protecting the Environment, US Environmental Protection Agency, Washington, DC. Available at *http://www.epa.gov/economics.*

European Commission (1997),
　　Tax Provisions with a Potential Impact on Environmental Protection, Luxembourg.

European Commission (1999),
　　Air transport and the environment: towards meeting the challenges of sustainable development. COM(1999)640. Available at *http://europa.eu.int/comm/transport/themes/air/english/library/environment_com_ %20en.pdf.*

Finish Economic Council (2000),
　　Environmental and Energy Taxation in Finland – Preparing for the Kyoto Challenge – Summary of the Working Group Report.

Gielen, D. and T. Kram (1998),
　　"The role of non-CO_2 greenhouse gases in meeting Kyoto targets", in Economic Modelling of Climate Change, OECD Workshop Report, 17-18 September.

Goulder, L. H., Parry, I. W. H., Williams III, R. C., and Burtaw, D. (1999),
　　The Cost-effectiveness of Alternative Instruments for Environmental Protection in a Second-Best Setting, *Journal of Public Economics,* 72, 329-360.

Harrison, D. Jr. (in OECD 1999),
　　Tradable permits for air pollution control: the US experience. Chapter II, OECD. Paris.

HM Treasury (1999a),
　　Economic and Fiscal Strategy Report. Her Majesty's Treasury, London. Available at *http://www.hm-treasury.gov.uk/budget/ 1999/index.html.*

HM Treasury (1999b),
　　Financial Statement and Budget Report. Her Majesty's Treasury, London. Available at *http://www.hm-treasury.gov.uk/ budget/1999/index.html*

Hoeller, P., Coppel, J. (1992),
　　Energy Taxation and Price Distortions in Fossil-fuel Markets: Some Implications for Climate Change Policy. In: OECD, Climate Change – Designing a Pracitcal Tax System. OECD, Paris.

Honkatukia (1997),
　　Are there Double Dividends in Finland? The Swedish Green Tax Commission Simulations for Finland, research report B:5, HKKK.

Honkatukia (2000),
　　Energiaverotuksen uudistamisen taloudelliset vaikutukset Suomesa, unpublished report to Economic Council secretariat.

IEA (1999a),
　　Energy Policies of IEA Countries, OECD/IEA, Paris.

IEA (1999b),
　　The Role of IEA Governments in Energy: 1999 Review, OECD/IEA, Paris.

IIMD (1996),
The World Competitiveness Yearbook, International Institute for Management Development, Lausanne.

IPCC (1999),
Special Report on Aviation and the Global Atmosphere: Summary for policymakers. IPCC, Geneva, Switzerland.

IRS (2000),
Excise Taxes for 2000. Publication 510. Internal Revenue Service, Washington, DC. Available at http://www.irs.gov/forms_pubs/pubs/p510toc.htm.

Jaffe, A., Peterson, S.R., Portney, P.R., Stavins, R.N. (1995),
"Environmental Regulation and the Competitiveness of US Manufacturing: What Does the Evidence Tell Us?" Journal of Economic Literature, Vol. XXXIII, March.

Jatzke, H.
"The ecological tax reform in Germany". Conference on Green tax reforms in Europe, 10th October 2000, Paris.

Kleijn, H. and J. Klooster (1990),
Het bewijs van de prijs. Ministerie van Verkeer en Waterstaat, Den Haag. In: European Commission (1997). Proposal for a Council Directive Restructuring the Community Framework for the Taxation of Energy Products, COM (97)30, Brussels.

Koopmans (1998),
Effects of National, OECD-wide and World-wide Energy Taxes on Environment and on competitiveness, in Barker and Köhler (eds.): International Competitiveness and Environmental Policies, Edward Elgar.

Larsen, Hans (2000),
Green Taxes – The Danish Experience, Ministry of Taxation, Copenhagen, Denmark. Presentation made at the conference "Supporting a Sustainable Future: Making Dollars and Sense", Vancouver, Canada, 11-13.12.2000. Available at http://www.ec.gc.ca/eco-n-ference/.

Larsen, B.M. and Nesbakken, R. (1997),
Norwegian Emissions of CO_2 1987-1994. "A Study of Some Effects of the CO_2 Tax", Environmental and Resource Economics, in course of publication.

Luhmann, H.J., Ell. R., Roemer, M. (1998),
"Unevenly distributed benefits from reducing pollutants, especially road traffic emissions, via reducing road transport." In: Environmental fiscal Reform – Final Report, Wuppertal.

Majocchi, A. (1996),
"Green Fiscal Reform and Employment: a Survey", Environmental and Resource Economics, Vol. 8, No. 4, December.

Majocchi, A. (2000),
Greening Tax Mixes in OECD Countries: A Preliminary Assessment, OECD, Paris. Available at http://www.oecd.org/env/policies/online-eco.htm.

Manne, A., R.G. Richels, E. Castelnouvo and M. Galeotti (2000),
A multi-gas approach to climate change policy -With and without GWPs. FEEM Working Paper No 44.2000.

Metcalf (1998),
A Distributional Analysis of an Environmental Tax Shift, NBER Working Paper 6546. Available at http://papers.nber.org/.

Miranda, Marie Lynn, Scott D. Bauer and Joseph E. Aldy (1995),
Unit Pricing Programs for Residential Municipal Solid Waste: An Assessment of the Literature. Report prepared for Office of Policy, Planning and Evaluation, US Environment Protection Agency. EE-0305. August. Available at http://www.epa.gov/economics.

Naturvårdsverket (1995),
Utvärdering av koldioxidskatten – har utsläppen av koldioxid minskat? Papport number 4512. Stockholm. In Swedish.

Nauges and Thomas (2000),
Estimation of Residential Water Demand, Land Economics, February, 76 (1)]. Nordhaus. W. D. (1994), Managing the global commons: The economics of climate change, MIT Press, Cambridge, MA (1994).

Nordic Council of Ministers (1999),
The Scope for Nordic Co-ordination of Economic Instruments in Environmental Policy, TemaNord, 1999-50.

OECD (1993),
Taxation and the Environment Complementary Policies, OECD, Paris.

OECD (1994),
The Distributive Effects of Economic Instruments for Environmental Policy, OECD, Paris.

OECD (1995a),
Environmental Taxes in OECD Countries, OECD, Paris.

OECD (1995*b*),
Environmental Principles and Concepts, OECD, Paris.

OECD (1996),
Implementation Strategies for Environmental Taxes, OECD, Paris.

OECD (1997),
Environmental Taxes and Green Tax Reform, OECD, Paris.

OECD (1997*b*),
Economic Globalisation and the Environment, OECD, Paris.

OECD (1997*c*),
Reforming Energy and Transport Subsidies: Environmental and Economic Implications, OECD, Paris.

OECD (1998),
Spotlight on Public Support to Industry, OECD, Paris.

OECD (1999*a*),
Voluntary Approaches for Environmental Policy: An Assessment, OECD, Paris.

OECD (1999*b*),
Taking Action Against Climate Change: The Kyoto Protocol, OECD, Paris.

OECD (1999*c*),
Agricultural Policies in OECD Countries: Monitoring and Evaluation, OECD, Paris.

OECD (1999*d*),
Implementing Domestic Tradable Permits for Environmental Protection – Proceedings, OECD, Paris.

OECD (1999*e*),
OECD Data, *Compendium 1999*. OECD, Paris.

OECD (2000*a*),
"Behavioural Responses to Energy and Transport-Related Taxes: A Survey of Price Elasticities Estimates", COM/ENV/EPOC/DAFFE/CFA(99)111/FINAL.

OECD (2000*b*),
"The Potential for Using Tax Instruments to Address Non-CO_2 Greenhouse Gases: CH_4, N_2O, HFCs, PFCs and SF_6, OECD, Paris. COM/ENV/EPOC/ DAFFE/CFA(99)110/FINAL.

OECD (2000*c*),
"Greening Tax Mixes In OECD Countries: A Preliminary Assessment", OECD, Paris. COM/ENV/EPOC/DAFFE/CFA(99)112/FINAL.

OECD (2000*d*),
The Impact on Fisheries Resource Sustainability of Government Financial Transfers, OECD, Paris.

Parry, I. W. H., Williams III, R. C., and Goulder, L. H. (1999),
When Can Carbon Abatement Policies Increase Welfare? The Fundamental Role of Distorted Factor Markets, *Journal of Environmental Economics and Management*, 37, 52-84.

Pearce, D.W., Cline, W.R., Achanta, A.N., Fankhauser, S., Pachauri, R.K., Tol, R.S.J., Vellinga, P. (1996),
The Social Costs of Climate Change: Greenhouse Damage and the Benefits of Control. In: IPCC, Climate Change 1995. Economic and Social Dimensions of Climate Change. Contribution of Working Group III to the 2nd Assessment Report of the IPCC. WMO and UNEP, Cambridge University Press, New York, NW, Chapter 6.

Pearce, D. and E.B. Barbier (2000),
Blueprint for a Sustainable Economy, Earthscan Publications Ltd, London.

Pigou, A.C. (1947),
A Study of Public Finance, 3rd ed. Macmillan, London.

Quota Commission (1999),
A quota system for greenhouse gases. A policy instrument for fulfilling Norway's emission reduction commitments under the Kyoto Protocol – Summary and recommendations. Norwegian Quota Commission, 1999. Available at *http://odin.dep.no/odinarkiv/norsk/dep/md/1999/eng/*.

Reilly, J., R. Prinn, J. Harnisch, J. Fitzmaurice, H. Jacoby, D. Kickligher, J. Melillo, P. Stone, A. Sokolov and C. Wang (1999),
"Multi-gas assessment of the Kyoto Protocol", *Nature*, Vol. 401, 7 October.

Repetto, R. (1996),
Shifting taxes from value added to material inputs. In: Carraro, C., Siniscalco, D. (Eds.), Environmental Fiscal Reform and Unemployment. Kluwer Academic Publishers, Dordrecht, The Netherlands, pp. 53-72.

RWI (Rheinisch-Westfälisches Institut für Wirtschaftsforschung) 1999 in Ecotec, (2000).

Sandmo, A. (1998),

"Redistribution and the marginal cost of public funds", Journal of Public Economics, 70, No. 3, pp 365-82.

Schlegelmilch, Kai (1997),

Green Tax Commissions, Environmental Policy Research Briefs, No. 4, The European Union.

Schlegelmilch, Kai (2000),

Ecological Tax Reform in Germany: Design and Experiences. Presentation made at the conference "Supporting a Sustainable Future: Making Dollars and Sense", Vancouver, Canada, 11-13.12.2000. Available at *http:// www.ec.gc.ca/eco-n-ference/*.

Schreiner, P. (1999),

Obstacles to the implementation of tradable permits: the case of Norway. Chapter VI, Implementing Domestic Tradable Permits for Environmental Protection – Proceedings, OECD, Paris.

Smith, Stephen (1998),

"Distributional Incidence of Environmental Taxes on Energy and Carbon: a Review of Policy Issues", presented at the colloquy of the Ministry of the Environment and Regional Planning, "Green Tax Reform and Economic Instruments for International Cooperation: the Post-Kyoto Context", Toulouse, 13 May 1998.

Smith, Stephen (1999),

The compatibility of tradable permits with other environmental policy instruments, Chapter X, Implementing Domestic Tradable Permits for Environmental Protection – Proceedings, OECD, Paris.

Snel, M. (2000),

"Green tax reform: the Dutch experience". Conference on Green tax reforms in Europe, 10th October 2000, Paris.

SOU (1997),

Skatter, miljö och sysselsättning – Slutbetenkande av Skatteväxlingskommitten, Statens offentliga utredningar 1997:11, Finansdepartement, Stockholm.

Swedish Environmental Protection Agency (1997),

Environmental Taxes in Sweden, Stockholm.

Symons and Proop, 1998 from ECOTEC study.

UK Round Table on Sustainable Development (2000),

Not too difficult! – Economic instruments to promote sustainable development within a modernised economy, London.

Umwelt-Gutachten (2000),

Schritte ins nächste Jahrtausend. Der Rat von Sachverstandigen für Umweltfragen.

Van Wee, B. (1995),

Pricing instruments for Transport Policy. In: Environment, Incentives and the Common Market, ed. F.J. Dietz, H.R.J. Vollebergh and J.L. de Vries, Kluwer Academic Publishers, the Netherlands.

Vermeed, W. and van der Vaart, J. (1998),

Greening Taxes: The Dutch Model, Kluwer, Deventer.

Walls, M. and Hanson, J. (1999),

"Distributional Aspects of an Environmental Tax Shift: The Case of Motor Vehicle Emissions Taxes", *National Tax Journal*, Volume LII, No.1: 53-65.